WHAT DID YOU DO IN THE WAR, DADDY?

How did you help us to win?

Dennis Berry

Published by Number 11 Publishing

D1218599

WHAT DID YOU DO IN THE WAR, DADDY?
How did you help us to win?

Copyright © Sandra Berry 2007

ISBN   978-0-9555134-1-1

Cover design and artwork, The Design Shop
www.thedesignshop.co.uk

Printed in England by www.printondemand-worldwide.com
Peterborough

First published 2007 by
Number 11 Publishing
PO Box 459
New Malden
Surrey KT3 9DH

www.number11publishing.co.uk

Printed in Great Britain for Number 11 Publishing

WHAT DID YOU DO IN THE WAR, DADDY?

How did you help us to win?

Dennis Berry

What did you do in the war, Daddy,
How did you help us to win?

Circuits and bumps and turns, laddy,
And how to get out of a spin!

Anonymous

NOTE

Dennis Berry wrote this, the first part of his autobiography, in the early 1990s following his second heart attack. In 2002, having survived for a further decade, he revised it. Dennis preferred to write rather than to wrangle with publishers, however, so his several books have remained in the computer until now.

Though I have taken the liberty of adding the photographs and running the Spell Check on *What Did You Do In The War, Daddy?*, at the end of the day this is what Dennis himself wrote about the most influential period of his full and varied life.

Sandra Berry
London
September 2007

John:
Thank you!
I trust that
you are both
keeping
well and
occupied.

11 Fairacre
Acacia Grove
NEW MALDEN
Surrey, KT3 3BS

www.number11publishing.co.uk

T: 020 8949 0159
E: sandra.berry@blueyonder.co.uk

Thank you for ordering

The Cobbold Elliston Affair.

I hope you enjoy it!

When are you
next coming
over ??

Cheers to
you and Nancy,
and I hope you enjoy
the read. (It is easier
than my book!)

With compliments

Sandra

Sergeant / Pilot Dennis Berry
RAF Desford, May 1943

CHAPTER I

1939

They had only two things in common, marrying into the same family and selling motorcars. Marrying sisters had brought them together in a way not otherwise possible, even though they worked in the same organisation. They were both excellent salesmen and although you would buy a motorcar from one of them out of conviction, from the other it would probably be against your better judgement - but you would buy it. Ernest Pritchard was brilliant in being able to sell you something by suggesting that you didn't want it. He was a psychologist, if that meant he understood human nature. His technique, I suppose, was to identify your interest and then appear indifferent to its satisfaction, until he had you hopping around selling the darn thing to yourself. It was a technique that required a lot of nerve, patience and acute observational ability. His pale blue eyes rarely showed emotion, but in the middle of a sale they would light up like the flags on a cash register.

Ronald Blackstock was slow, warm and honest. If he said it was a 'good buy' you could take his word for it. And it was not a sales pitch either, he really was honest.

Ernest Pritchard took his work home with him, evenings, weekends, everywhile. His constant conniving and planning preoccupied him totally, so that he would sit sometimes physically with, but mentally remote from, the family doings. They never complained. His guests, and he entertained extensively, never complained either, for he was a very generous host and always attentive. He would study them all closely, for might not one or other of them be of use to him in his business? This possibility became the major determinant in the choice of friends, leading sometimes to rather odd weekends for the family.

Ron Blackstock played golf.

The Pritchards lived in a comfortable red-tiled house on the London Road into Sittingbourne, which at that time was no worse

1

than the other Medway towns. Traffic through the High Street only became objectionable at weekends when the east coast holidaymakers fussed by, nose to tail. Apart from that, Sittingbourne was still a community with its WI, the Odeon on the corner and cricket on the Rec. Half the town seemed to work at the Paper Mill, that smelly and black Victorian pile which hissed and fumed just behind the High Street. Edward Lloyd's Paper Mill was still a family business much closer in spirit to Charles Dickens than to any modern enterprise. Old Mr Denny, thick pince-nez below his beetle brows and bald pate, bent over his books with his chewed briar belching smoke like the factory's chimney, <u>was</u> the Paper Mill. He, and a few fusty clerks like him, despatched those great drums of newsprint up to the Street and to elsewhere. This, of course, was all before the Americans moved in and closed them down and before the traffic planners slashed their roads through the little Victorian terraces and carved up the town forever.

The Blackstocks lived in the country, in a newly-built half-timbered house set in pine trees and called Tree-Tops. They rarely entertained. Tree-Tops was a retreat, a retreat from the world which had to be tolerated only from 9.0 to 5.0. Bearsted was a chocolate box village and like all good chocolates its inhabitants were well insulated from each other, wrapped in layers of respectability.

The war came like the end of the school holidays, a nightmare, although a nightmare everyone expected and were relieved therefore when it at last started. For Ernest Pritchard it was all grossly unfair and not according to plan at all. He had opened his first garage a year earlier at Chalkwell, built with borrowed money – a brittle, Crittal-windowed, white Art Deco palace with its concrete forecourt furnished with second-hand cars. And then the war came.

It was on Friday 1st of September, a beautiful hot summer's day, when the German blitzkrieg smashed into Poland invoking Chamberlain's pledge to defend the Poles if they were attacked. The screaming Stukas hammering Guernica off the map of Spain had already been seen in the newsreels and Ernest Pritchard's wife, or my sister Rene as I should now identify her, prevailed upon him to send two cars up to London to evacuate the family - Mum, Dad, brother

2

Vic, his wife Doreen and me, the baby of the family. We all piled into the two cars, plus the food from the larder and the sheets and blankets bundled off the beds.

We arrived in Sittingbourne to be immediately, and willingly, directed to finish digging the air raid shelter in the garden. Although underneath the flight path of the subsequent nightly bomber streams on their way to London, this shelter was never used in anger. However, on that sky-blue day of impending disaster, the activity although arduous was therapeutic.

Chamberlain's heartbroken broadcast on the Sunday morning when he announced "This country is now at war with Germany. We are ready." was like the opening of a door to doom. Everyone dreaded the awful demons which must come pouring out.

Half an hour later, the air raid sirens wailed and we scanned the eastern sky with dread looking for the first squadrons of Stukas we fully expected. But it was a false alarm and no hordes of bombers appeared that day.

It was to be many months in fact before the demons of war did emerge and long before this we had returned, a bit sheepishly perhaps, to London. Brother-in-law Ernest meanwhile, faithful to his own beliefs, sought to turn the war to his advantage. He bought a fleet of lorries and then drummed up work transporting war supplies to and fro, such as fruit from the Kent apple orchards. After all, people were not buying cars at that time and he had to keep his garage afloat. Ron, my other brother-in-law, who had joined Ernest as partner and co-director in the new garage venture, had a conscience however about the war. He spoke to EGP, as Ernest was known by everyone in the garage, one afternoon to tell him that he was going to join up.

"Don't be daft man. We've got to keep this place on its feet. I've got every penny tied up in it and I'm not going to be put out of business by this bloody war."

"You can keep Chalkwell going without me, Ernie, and it will help if I'm not taking out a salary." Ron Blackstock tamped out his enormous Dunhill in the burn-stained Bakelite ashtray on the desk in front of him.

"And the war will be won without your help too. Don't be daft man."

But the argument about saving a salary had registered and Ernest began to look thoughtful.

"There is only one thing Ernie, if I do go off I want to be sure that Vie and young Michael are OK."

Ernest stubbed out a half-smoked Players. "You must do whatever you think best Ron. I think you are a fool, but whatever you decide, don't worry about Vie and Mike. I promise I'll look after them." How easy it is to tell someone that which they most want to hear. So, Ron Blackstock went off to the war leaving Ernest to fight his own private version.

We received regular news of Ron's progress from my sister. He had volunteered for aircrew in the RAF which, while invoking my envy, had filled everyone else with dismay. Ron had always shared my teenage passion for flying and encouraged it by giving me model aeroplane kits to assemble. The prize one of these I remember as a lad of 14 had been the model of a Hawker Fury, the front line fighter of the RAF. It was a beautiful model, in hardwood, with the thinnest wing sections imaginable and decorated with the red and white checker pattern of the relevant squadron. Ron, then in his early 20s, had obviously felt something of my enthusiasm when he first held the model. It exemplified the beauty of the real thing, only to be excelled by its successor when it arrived, the fabulous Hurricane. It was no wonder to me that my 'friend' had volunteered to fly such creations.

Ron was 28 when he swung his leg over the side of a Tiger Moth for the first time, an old man compared with the lads in his flight. Perhaps this was the most telling factor against him in the race to go solo. He was a cautious type by nature and while he had all the necessary skills to master flight, to get that contraption down on the grass in one piece he needed time to relax and to perfect the operation. Time was not available however. The RAF, driven by necessity, expected cadets to solo in less than a dozen hours. Ron was washed out from the course and chose to remuster as a wireless operator. He spent the rest of his war manning radar posts on the coast of Kent, plotting the paths of the raiders he had hoped to meet face to face. At least he survived the war that way.

1940

The weather remained gorgeous, hot and sunny well into a late-arriving autumn, reassuring both farmers and politicians alike. The children, evacuated from London in such panic, began to drift back and Christmas seemed quite normal in terms of puddings and presents, but underlying everything was an oppressive sense of unease. "Things must hot up soon", they said, looking up at the clear blue sky.

And, of course, they did. In April the war exploded when Hitler overran Denmark and then invaded Norway with much bloody fighting. A month later his Panzers swept unstoppable through Belgium and Holland. Chamberlain finally gave way, broken and defeated and Churchill took over as the rearguard action began to develop around Dunkirk. When Belgium capitulated on the 28th May the military disaster he had inherited seemed complete and the evacuation of the British Expeditionary Force began. The armada of little boats plied the Channel to bring home an army without guns, thus elevating the disaster of Dunkerque into some sort of victory.

On 22 June, at the Forest of Compiegne and in the same railway coach that General Foch in 1918 had thrust his armistice terms upon the Germans, Hitler now humiliated the French. His dance of joy after the signing of the armistice, recorded for all time on newsreel, is an icon of his megalomania.

This was the darkest hour, which Churchill magically illuminated. His "thousand years" speech still sends tingles down my spine now, half a century later. At the time it was pure inspiration for we besieged British. Even Mussolini's declaration of war at this time was greeted more with grimness than fear. Indeed, it was a very grim Churchill who, shortly after his assumption of leadership, ordered the sinking of the French fleet in Algiers lest it be used by the enemy against us, even though this cost the lives of a thousand French sailors. It was the action of a resolute realist, the man for the hour.

The summer of 1940 was idyllic with life continuing much unchanged except for some brooding sense of impending calamity. In preparation for his invasion of the British Isles - the next conquest on his agenda, having mopped up the rest of Europe - Hitler ordered Göring to smash the RAF as a preliminary to invasion. His plan began with aerial attacks on shipping in the Channel, not only to cut off our supplies but also to lure the planes of Fighter Command up into a battle Göring was confident his Messerschmitts would win. After all, had they not already vanquished Europe from Spain to Poland, spearheading Hitler's invincible Panzers? When the shipping convoys were eventually withdrawn from the Channel, because of this bombing, the Luftwaffe transferred its attacks to the Kent airfields and to the radar masts in the south east of England. The Battle of Britain had begun.

Sometimes it seemed that the battle was centred directly overhead, its progress marked by drifting con-trails and scored with a soundtrack of tortured aero-engines and staccato gunfire. It was usually at heights where the combatants were not visible, only the scream of the engines and the con-trails identified their presence and an occasional necklace of smoke puffs followed seconds later by the cough of the slower German cannon fire. Then occasionally an inverted rocket of smoke would fall earthwards to mark someone's defeat.

On one such day watching the remote aerial display, I saw a falling object, silvery and twisting like a leaf. I remember shrieking out for mother to come and see. We watched it, convinced we were seeing a German plane falling. As it got quite close to the ground, just beyond the trees, we saw the RAF roundel.

On other occasions we would watch a parachute coming down, long after the sudden rush of battle had passed. Whether these were German or British airmen one could never tell.

Ron was in the front line of this war, not where he had hoped to be up there in the sky, but in a gloomy Nissan Hut, intent over a cathode ray tube, plotting the 'bandits' as they flew towards the chalk cliffs of Kent.

The news would have it that we were winning the battle, always with heavy German losses. Little did the public know just how close we were coming to defeat that midsummer and just how few allied airmen there were to stop Hitler in his world conquest. It was not until many years after the war that the historians were to tell us about the petty jealousies which existed between the Commanders of 11 and 12 Groups, the regional massing of squadrons north and south of the Thames. 11 Group maintained that squadrons operating from the Northern sector should not penetrate South unless they came under the direction of 11 Group. This was resisted by 12 Group with the result that even when faced by overwhelming odds 11 Group was too often denied help from the fresh Northerly squadrons. Perhaps the Battle need not have been the close run fight it was had the Commander of Fighter Command, Air Chief-Marshal Sir Hugh Dowding, knocked the two Group Commander's heads together for their infantile behaviour! Another disquieting fact also emerged later, about the astonishing authority a mere Squadron Leader in 12 Group had upon the Battle. Douglas Bader, the legless wonder, advocated the use of large wings of fighters being sent up to confront the invading bombers rather than the much less numerous groupings Dowding preferred for the tactic of flexibility of response. The resulting conflict between the two Groups was not helped by Bader's advocacy which Leigh-Mallory, the Air Officer Commanding 12 Group, supported. Allowing too many cooks in the kitchen in this way must detract slightly from Dowding's otherwise magnificent leadership. These views of the Battle in hindsight, however, cannot alter the overall tremendous achievement of Dowding and his pilots, although at the time his reward was the sack and expulsion to America!

Perhaps at the end of the day Göering did as much to defeat himself as did the RAF, for it is now known that had he continued bombing the airfields for just a few more days, the RAF could scarcely have been able to defend any further. As it was, Hitler, incensed by a small raid on Berlin threatened to reduce London to rubble and Göering was ordered to switch from attacking the airfields to bombing the capital city.

I had gone to the Capitol Cinema at Forest Hill that Saturday afternoon in September, with two of the girls, Edna and Evelyn. Edna was in love with me I believe, but not me with her. She had a squint, poor girl, whereas Evelyn was much more interesting. Unfortunately, she was not interested in me. Life can be chronic! We sat at the back of the stalls enjoying the film, when across the screen flashed a message "There is an air raid warning. Please stay in your seats." The film continued, but with the house lights up and amidst a general buzz of conversation no one was really watching it anymore. A second message came on the screen - "Our roof observer has seen an enemy plane shot down." A great cheer went up from the audience. Further messages were flashed up reporting the progress of what sounded like a victorious battle overhead.

Suddenly there was a great 'whoomph' and the cinema seemed to shake. People rose in their seats and started pushing out to the aisles. Then, impelled by the acute sense of panic which seemed to be developing, but more in a sense of self-preservation than bravado, I climbed on to the arms of my seat and raising my hands I shouted at the people in front of me, "Sit down, for God's sake sit down. We are safe in here."

Probably in spite of my gesture, the audience shuffled back and sat down again. The panic could have developed and many people could have been hurt in the process, but whether my intervention was really influential, or not, is questionable, but I like to think it was!

When the all-clear was given, we left the cinema. There were no signs of the anticipated devastation outside, however, so we walked back to the Horniman Museum and turned into the Park. It was still daylight and from the top of the hill we could see across London. Huge billowing clouds of black smoke were rising from the East End, from the docks, the City and from Woolwich, where 300 bombers, escorted by twice as many fighters had come up the Thames to drop their loads. Two hours later another 250 bombers appeared to stoke the fires already started.

The attacks continued during the night up to 4.0 am and as London suffered so Hugh Dowding breathed his relief. The pressure was no longer on the airfields - the Battle of Britain had been won!

That night of the 7th September was the first of many sleepless ones for us. With darkness came the stomach-churning wail of the air raid sirens, followed by the crisp thump, thump, thump of ack ack fire. Then, the ominous noise of the unsynchronised engines of the bombers. By now we would be down in the cellar, trying to gain comfort from its notional security and trying not to think of the house collapsing over us, just as we had seen in so many newsreels in the cinema.

"How long can we keep this up?" my mother asked.

"As long as it takes, I guess. There's not much we can do about it is there?" Dad's face was a little greyer than usual perhaps as he checked the earth-filled sack up in front of the cellar window. The decision was ultimately removed from us however, by the bomb which fell across the road. While not a direct hit on our house it did remove most of its roof and blew in the front door and all the windows.

So, once more a fleet of cars came up from Sittingbourne to evacuate the family and to give us some much needed night's sleep. Only this time we never returned to London and by Christmas we were safely housed next door to my sister.

Christmas 1940 began to show the effects of the war. There were carrots instead of dried fruit in the pudding, no bananas anymore, and oranges, lemons and onions were just a memory. But this was hardly disasterville!

1941

By now I had met a girl in Sittingbourne and I would be 19 in the February of 1941 and therefore eligible for service. Shortly after Christmas, Joan and I went into an RAF recruiting office in Chatham where I volunteered for flying duties. I had to wait until March, however, before I heard anything when I was summoned to Uxbridge - for aircrew selection - the paper said.

It was the worst three days of my life. I spent hours queuing, with dozens of others, stripped to the waist and in bare feet, padding from one medical test to the next. Eyes, ears, lungs, heart and other parts of my body were probed, measured, tested and sampled. One heart stopping moment was when sitting back against a wall the length of my legs were measured. I knew that a minimum was necessary to be able to reach the controls in a cockpit and with a height of only 5' 8" I knew I must be borderline. I only just made it, apparently, and passed on relieved to the next test.

The second day was given over to written tests which included psychological subjects such as spatial and verbal reasoning, and on to educational ones like geometry and mathematics. It was the maths paper which nearly washed me out. I got it badly wrong apparently and finished up in front of three very senior Air Officers. They told me that I was one hundred per cent fit, with A1 eyesight and therefore eligible for Pilot Training - but for this silly maths paper.

"What went wrong here? Didn't you understand the question?" The acres of gold braid and the chests of medal ribbons under the magical wings swam before my eyes. I was half paralysed with fright. I mumbled something and one of the great men thrust a paper and pencil across the desk at me. "Work that out then."

I stared at the equation on the paper. It was like a nightmare. Now, fifty years on, and I can still recapture that moment as if it were months ago. Aware of the three officers glowering over me I picked up the pencil ... and by some inspired and superhuman effort I wrote down the answer. The Air Commodore looked at it, looked up at me and then smiled. "Fine. Why didn't you do that in the first place?"

They told me I was accepted for Pilot Training and that I would be called up shortly. It was the greatest moment of my life. Mum and Dad were less than happy though, while they could not deny me my achievement, nor fail to recognise my joy ... I was after all just their baby, and it was all so dangerous. Joan at least was proud of me. None of the other girls had a fighter pilot as a boy friend and as for the danger, well - it added zest to life.

CHAPTER 2

The next four months passed with a nerve-tensioning build-up until the morning the official looking letter actually arrived wherein I was instructed to report to the Air Crew Reception Centre at Regents Park on the 14th July. The good-byes on the platform at Chatham Station were harrowing enough with everyone crying, although for me, I know it was not half as bad as it was for those I was leaving behind. I was going off to start the adventure of my life, but for Mum and Dad - it was their baby going off to war, and I could not at that stage really understand their grief. My mother was quite desolate and Dad could find no words to comfort her, such, I suspect, was his own misery. It seemed as if Vic was seeing me, his young brother, for the first time. We had never been great friends, but this situation somehow highlighted our relationship and he felt an unfamiliar protectiveness for me.

The train puffed smokily out of the station and I remember sitting back feeling suddenly very lonely and a shade scared. I tried not to think of their white faces turned towards me as the train pulled away from the platform. This was the first time I had ever left home. But this was what I had wanted. "For God's sake, think of the future." I chided myself.

My experience on arrival at the No 2 Receiving Wing at Regents Park was chaotic, but slightly ameliorated by the presence of dozens of other similarly bewildered young men and among whom an immediate camaraderie developed. We even began to mutter like old lags as we were herded together into Flights of fifty. My Flight, 19/3, was finally shuffled off, an odd assortment of men with each one carrying his possessions in his suitcase, along Prince Albert Road to some unfinished blocks of flats. Here, we were detailed by a corporal, five to a room, where we found blankets piled in the corner and were told, "This is where you kip." Brick rubble littered the floor and had to be 'shoed' to one side before the blankets could be spread. The windows were unglazed and the whole set-up was obviously a temporary billet, or so we hoped.

From here, having dumped our suitcases, we were immediately 'marched' back to a Pavilion in the park, apparently borrowed from the Zoo. This was the cookhouse and they lined us up to collect a meal we were told was called Tea. It was quite inedible. Something, presumably meat, floated in brown grease along with two dollops of, I think, mashy potato and the pudding was a two-inch cube of something rubbery in unsweetened custard. It was difficult to identify the ingredients. The cooks might just as well have poured everything straight into the trash bins and saved on the washing up for the amount that was eaten.

I spent thirteen miserable days at 'Arcy Darcy' (Aircrew Reception Centre), doing very little other than marching up and down Regent's Park Road and to and fro the cookhouse. The public lined up outside the railings of the park to watch the airmen feeding, much as they watched the monkeys further up the road. It was questionable as to which was the greater entertainment for them, the airmen or the monkeys!

For the first two of the thirteen days we still wore our civilian clothes, but then on the third day we were kitted out with uniforms and kitbags to keep everything in. The amount of kit was overwhelming, including a tunic, trousers and a forage cap, a tin helmet, boot brushes, boots, gas mask, greatcoat, cape, webbing, haversacks, irons (knife, fork and spoon) and a jack-knife with tin opener! The novelties of the kit included the brass button stick which enabled one to clean the buttons without getting Brasso all over the uniform, and the 'hussif', or 'housewife' - a kit of needles, threads and spare buttons. There was also the white flash which tucked into the front of the forage cap distinguishing the aircrew cadet from the ordinary airman. This was the first of the badges we young men were to receive, marking us out as an elite group in an elite service. Another such badge came with the uniform, the small pale blue VR insignia to be worn at the top of the sleeves. VR stood for Volunteer Reserve, the category of service which replaced the peacetime Auxiliary Air

12

Force, the force which provided many of the Battle of Britain pilots. No airman was ever posted to flying duties, for all aircrew were volunteers.

Pass-outs were issued but with a restricted radius of five miles and a book-in time of 10.30 pm, or 2230 hours. This at least permitted some escape from the tedium allowing a visit perhaps to the Odeon at Swiss Cottage, or a milk bar, or pub in Camden Town, depending upon your tastes. A most memorable film and a marvellous tonic was 'That Night in Rio' with Carmen Miranda, her hair full of fruit, singing:

"I, Yi, Yi, Yi, Yi I Like You Very Much.
I, Yi, Yi, Yi, Yi I think you're grand."

It was a bit better suited to everyone's mood than that tedious nightingale singing currently in Berkeley Square!

Another afternoon we were marched off to the same cinema only this time to listen to the medical officer talk about the dangers of VD - I thought how it too could have been entertaining had he also worn a bowl of fruit on his head. As it was, I slept through the really exciting bits.

There were seven thousand men at any one time in the Receiving Wing, staying for periods of up to three weeks, being kitted out, inoculated, vaccinated, sorted and then posted for training. It would have been miraculous to have run such an enterprise without a few hiccoughs. One of the problems was keeping all of these men occupied while they were being processed. This responsibility fell primarily upon the NCOs and particularly on the Corporal in charge of each Flight. Mostly these men were gems and justified the respect they usually received. I wrote home about the quality of the NCOs, saying how marvellous they were,

"Very kindly, helpful, paternal even. Corporal Claridge gave us a heart to heart talk the other day, very worldly and to the point. And all this was on his own initiative. Nothing to do with the system."

As I remember, it was far more to the point than the Medical Officer's earlier effort on the same subject. The day started with reveille at 0600 hours, followed by washing, cleaning and sweeping the room and setting out the kit for inspection. Parade was at 0715 hours for breakfast in the Zoo, a mile away. Then more cleaning and sweeping, followed by drill, drill, drill. Oh, my poor blistered feet. The next parade was for lunch, followed by more drill, or a lecture if the weather was wet. Then the Tea parade, after which we were free at 1800 hours, provided we were not on guard, or fire picket duty. I reckoned that we probably marched somewhere between ten and, on a bad day, twenty miles.

The food was not so bad, I suppose, considering all things and many civilians were doing much worse at this time. Breakfast consisted of a cereal, followed by bacon, or scrambled egg on toast (dried egg that is), or bangers, usually with potatoes; lunch of meat, potatoes, peas or beans or carrots, bread or date pudding, figs, or fruit pie; tea of peas pudding and savaloys, or sausages, or cheese and pickles and always with bread, margarine and jam. The trouble was that it was all ruined in the cooking and serving and the tea was laced with so much bromide (as rumour had it) as to be almost undrinkable.

I wrote home following the receipt of my first food parcel, "The home cooking in your parcel was just what the doctor ordered. You needn't send any more butter though as I had some from Rene which I have not used up yet. Don't think I'm starving, you know. We have plenty of grub and in addition the Church Army Canteen comes round about twice a day with buns and tea. It is really the small cakes and tarts that are most acceptable as a snack before bed. The custard tarts are delicious and I try to ration myself rigidly to make them last out."

Letters from home were the major event of life, as they must have been for every serviceman away from home - these and the food parcels. I wrote: "Rouse everyone up to write to me, even if I don't write back."

Being confined to camp until evening and without access to the wireless, news was scarce and this prompted me to add, "Short of news up here. I would be glad if you could tell me of any startling tit-bits on the wireless you hear, like if we win the war, or anything. I should hate to miss it!"

After the first few days of suffering and sleeping in the unfinished building, we were moved into better accommodation, indeed luxury flats with a bathroom to every room and running hot and cold. I moved with the two men I had already chummed up with, Jimmy, a policeman from Deal and '2 Pair', a Welshman so called because he got away with two pairs of everything at kitting out. '2 Pair' had played forward for Bristol first eleven and Corporal Claridge we learnt was also a Rugger International.

By the end of the fortnight we were marching about with some orderliness, our blistered feet and ankles beginning to harden inside the unforgiving boots and the lads beginning to feel like airmen. What a blessing, although perhaps not fully appreciated at the time - this was a lovely summer. How miserable it could have been to experience ACRC in a wet November!

We were finally moved into the Posting Wing and I wrote home: "Things are in a lousy state - no organisation at all. I did attend a lecture on Morse today, but that is all we have yet done, except to stand about and have our name and number taken at periods of 10 - 20 minutes and having different COs and NCOs chivvying us from one place to another. The raid here on Monday was very noisy, but we had no bombs near us. I lay in bed with my tin helmet on. I expect you know more about the raid than I do?"

At long last notice was given that on the morrow we would all be posted away from this hellhole to begin our training at an Initial Training Wing. I felt a double delight when I learnt that I was going to Number 4 ITW at Paignton, in Devon. It was at the seaside!

A few days after the miserable good-byes on Chatham Station I gather that Dad found Mum in tears. I had been sending my soiled underclothes home from London for laundering as such facilities were non-existent in Regent's Park. Unfortunately Mum had found the plugs of bloodstained cotton wool in my socks, which I had used to protect the blisters on my feet and had forgotten to remove. What were mere irritants really to me at the time became near mortal wounds to mother. It worried her desperately as she imagined her son marching about in agony with his boots awash with blood.

Life, however, for my family left in Sittingbourne apparently had become reasonably established although the news from home arrived as if from another planet. For nineteen years my view of the world had been an introspective one from inside the family palisade. Now, it seemed, as if I was outside and looking in at the family and with a very personal palisade which surrounded me alone. It made, strangely, a feeling of security.

The news was that my Father and Vic had rented a lock-up shop in the High Street, just before Pullen's garage opposite East Street, and set up the dual business of a cycle shop and a bookmaker's establishment. The cycle business was founded on the residue of the shop Dad had vacated in Dulwich on being bombed out, while the bookmaking was a continuation of Vic's London activity. It was always assumed that the tensions his early gambling induced were responsible for his duodenal ulcers which ultimately made him unfit for military service!

Of the two industries, cycling and bookmaking, there is no doubt as to which was the more successful. Although theoretically, with the war, cycling had come into its own, Vic's knowledge of the horses and his skill with numbers made him a natural but, more importantly, very successful bookmaker. This is not to say that Dad failed in any way. Indeed, trade was adequate and the cycle business paid the rent. It was simply that Vic was extremely successful - but it was only a small shop which precluded expansion for either of them and physical expansion was of more importance to the cycle business than it was to bookmaking, if Dad was ever to make a go of it.

As time went on, father and son became both well-known and popular figures in the local community. They were easy-going, likeable personalities, always ready to jolly a customer along and to appear interested in his problems - and that is always good business.

At long last, on 27th July 1941, my flight was transported from Regent's Park to St Pancras Station, to entrain for Devon. It was a great day. We all felt and even looked like airmen. With the magic flash in our caps, we could march, advance, halt - 1 2 3 4 - salute, about turn and march back again, all with metronomic regularity. We had queued up for our inoculations and had watched the men in front keel over without fainting ourselves. And now we were off to begin the real adventure, to learn how to become pilots. Had we known about the rigours ahead, perhaps we might have been less sanguine.

CHAPTER 3

The train drew in to that curious station platform across Paignton High Street, its ice cream parlours, picture postcards and teashops going off at right angles. We airmen were, as they say, 'fell in', on the sand-blown roadway to march to our billet. This was the Palace Hotel, slap-bang on the front, with a large expanse of grass to one side of it and the blue-grey sea in front of it. Our reception at the Hotel was impressive, in notable contrast with that in London. A Corporal, with a mouth which must have been the inspiration for Mick Jagger's, took us into his care, briefed us and allocated us to our rooms. We were three to a room it appeared, each of which was furnished with sprung iron beds on which were three square mattresses (to become known as biscuits), four blankets, two sheets and a pillow. The sheets were a luxury no one had expected, as was the lavatory basin with hot and cold water.

A cupboard stood at the side of each bed with a chart pasted up inside its door showing how kit had to be laid out. The floor was covered with polished lino in which the legs of the beds reflected as if from still water. It all looked so much more organised than Regent's Park, thank heavens!

Having dumped our kit we were told to parade outside the front of the hotel. The Corporal stood us to attention and then marched with parade ground precision up to a Flight Sergeant, before whom he stood with exaggerated rigidity, thumbs straining down the seams of his trousers.

"A Flight, all present and correct, Flight Sergeant", he bellowed, to the possible relief of the landladies in Torquay.

If the Corporal was a native of Bermondsey, the Flight Sergeant probably came from Bow. They shouted at each other in raucous Cockney, using parade ground jargon, at the end of which the Flight Sergeant in turn marched up to an Officer and went through the "All present and correct, Sir" bit. He was told to stand the Flight at ease and the Squadron Leader then gave us the programme for the next six weeks – he said. He told us that we would alternate mornings and afternoons with lectures, and drill and PT. The lectures would cover signals, both Wireless Telegraphy and Aldis Lamp, armaments, aircraft recognition, theory of flight, maths and navigation. The maths would last for the first two weeks and would then be examined, with failure immediately washing out from the course. All of the lecture subjects were to be examined finally and a pass in everything was required for promotion on to flying training. Rumour had it that Navigation was the real tough one. After my experience at Uxbridge, however, the maths exam was the one that worried me. The other bad news was that reveille was at 0600 hours every morning, parade at 0700 and lectures, or PT, at 0800. The day was scheduled to end at 1800 hours with supper at 1900. Evenings were said to be free, free that is after the necessary quota of study, button cleaning, boot polishing and always provided one was not on guard duty, which came round apparently about once a week. One had to book in by 2130 hours and 'lights out' was at 2230.

The good news was that all lectures were in the hotel and that we would also eat there, the catering being done by the YMCA. The Squadron Leader stressed the quality of No 4 ITW, "This is the most prestigious ITW in the country. You walk out in your free time wearing the ceremonial belt and with that flash in your cap. Woe betide anyone brought before me who lets that uniform down. He will be immediately dismissed off the course."

Six, or so, weeks of physical training and 'square bashing' was bound to have an effect. At the end of the period I, like most of the cadets, had never before been as fit. A twenty-mile route march with full pack left me relatively indifferent and at the end there was very little the PT instructor could do to faze us. We actually enjoyed the drill, exulting in the crisp precision we were achieving where fifty men went through a complex manoeuvre with the sound of a single pistol shot rather than a drum roll. We grumbled of course, sweating cobs in the midsummer heat, swearing to leave our Corporal emasculated -

slowly, one at a time, and with a blunt kitchen knife - but perversely revelling in our agonies.

On one occasion the Corporal marched us to a quiet residential road at the back of Paignton, halted us by the pavement and then addressed us in his parade ground voice so that the entire street could hear,

"There's a woman who lives not a million miles away from here who's got VD. And she likes young airmen. She's not worth it though. The clap is too big a price to pay."

It was rough justice to mete out to the woman in question, but we were very impressed. A lot of the lads were certainly out in the evenings looking for it among the visiting holidaymakers. One of my roommates came in one evening on the stroke of 2130 sweating and very flushed, and also very drunk. He boasted of how he had just had this girl up against an air raid shelter. I was too tired to be impressed. I was even less impressed when soon after lights out, he got out of bed, urinated in one of his boots and climbed back into bed. I enjoyed the following morning, however, hearing him 'left, squelch, left,' on the parade ground.

Corporal Wilson's persona was larger than life. He was the classical stereotype of all military NCOs, gruff, rough, threatening and yet really a softy with a great Cockney sense of humour. He was to coax, bully, wheedle and threaten we naive young men through the next, and toughest weeks of our lives. There was nothing in the Air Force Manual about why and how he should do it; it just came naturally. Like Ernest Pritchard, he was a quasi-psychologist and he knew how to influence people.

The maths were worrying, with my differential equations very shaky. I spent every evening revising that day's lecture and working out examples. But, miraculously, I made it in the exam, although a couple of the cadets were washed out. Navigation thereafter did not seem so bad. Signals were more of a problem, especially with the Aldis Lamp. Although we only had to receive five words a minute with the Aldis and transmit at 6, and were already up to 7 and 8, the lamp was so ponderous somehow and we all dreaded the exam. It was relatively easy for two of us to sit down and 'dit..dit..dit..da..dit' away to each other, but quite another thing to go on opposite sides of the green and clonk away with the Aldis.

Aircraft recognition soon became a bore. Sitting in a dark lecture room trying to recognise the silhouettes of aeroplanes as they were flashed on the screen, was a recipe for dozing. The lecturer countered this by occasionally flashing up a disgustingly lewd photograph and we had to stay awake in case we missed it each time. "Look at those twin engines ... I'd give her a daily service anytime ... Imagine doing circuits and bumps on that ... You'd never last the course ..."

Armaments were also unpopular, mainly because the subject seemed to have little relevance to we embryonic pilots. Of what use was it to know how to clear a blockage in a .303 Browning when the only time it would happen would be in the wing of a Spitfire at 20,000 feet? "Far better to tell us how to launder our pants," someone said.

Guard duty was a novel experience - at first. One only had to stand guard for two hours and then one slept fully dressed in the guardroom for the rest of the night. The rifle was loaded and with its fixed bayonet it was a lethal weapon in the hands of these naive airmen. There was much speculation as to what one did if the guard's challenge brought forth the answer "Foe." Did you shoot straight away, or merely bayonet the advancing stranger? And if it were the Flight Sergeant you happened to kill, would that be enough to wash you out?

The war, although seemingly a long way away from Paignton, was warming up. Hitler's invasion of Russia, begun on 30th June just before my call-up, had by now made huge gains in territory. The Russians were retreating on a vast front from the Baltic to the Black Sea, but in the process they were absorbing Hitler's war machine without conceding anything other than scorched earth. By the end of August, the Germans were reported to be fighting within thirty miles of Leningrad and the advance on Moscow itself was also being heavily reinforced. For us, sunning by the seaside while we prepared to take our part in the conflict, the war seemed a long way away. The more frivolous would say, "Let's hope it lasts until we get there.."

This period gave the Allies the desperately-needed time to re-equip the remnants of the army brought back from the humiliation of Dunkirk and to regroup the exhausted squadrons which had won the Battle of Britain. It was still a grim period, however, for the people at home. Rationing was now extended to clothing and everyone with a garden patch or an allotment was busily 'Digging for Victory'. If the mood of the people was grim, it was also determined. As a friend of mine once wrote to me, "I think this 'V for Victory' campaign is redundant. Hell, we know we are going to win."

There were five men in my immediate family and of these two were already in the forces. A third, my brother Vic, was unfit to serve and dad was too old. This left Ernest, but there was never any question of him going to war. He did say once that the boys in the services had to have jobs to come back to and he probably thought he would like to be in a position to provide them. He certainly never felt it morally necessary to defend himself for keeping out of the war. He had two brothers, one older and one younger, who both went in to the Royal Engineers and both of whom he employed on demobilisation. And no one could say that Ernest did not work extremely hard during the war. He was sometimes up at 4.30 am to load and deliver fruit up to the markets.

It was about this time that a customer started talking to him about Freemasonry. The idea of joining a brotherhood and gaining perhaps some protection thereby in this hostile world obviously appealed to him. There was also the entrée it offered to a potential host of new customers. This was not openly boasted of course, but tacitly understood - and why not - there is nothing wrong in honest business, is there?

The Pennys were entertained and Jim Penny closely questioned about the arcane mysteries of the brotherhood. "Why do you go along with it? What do you get out of it?"

"Ernest, it isn't a question of getting something out of it. Freemasonry is all about putting something in." Ernest shook his head.

Jim Penny was a businessman too and he well understood what Ernest Pritchard was saying. He also liked the idea of introducing a new candidate into the Lodge.

"Ernest, Freemasonry is a society with secrets and I cannot tell you about these. What I can say is that Freemasonry is an honourable institution and that its purposes are charitable. It is a great brotherhood and, yes, we do look after our own." This last bit was what Ernest wanted to hear.

He was duly initiated and the reality of Freemasonry, which one must say disappointed many, hooked him like a drug. To a man otherwise without religion, or any other profound beliefs, the secrets of Freemasonry appealed almost sensuously. He served in the lower offices with proper humility and eventually, as Master, with dignity, gracing the office and earning praise from the elders of the Lodge. Ernest served Freemasonry well and Freemasonry in return served him. For example, there was that spot of trouble with the ministry over some invoices where 'fraudulent dealings' was being whispered. It never got to court - thanks to Freemasonry as some malicious people suggested. It did leave a nasty odour for some time though and many wondered how he could still be a member of a so-called honourable society. Similar things have been said about Catholics of course. Absolution granted at the confessional does not stop them from going off and committing the same sin all over again. Not that Ernest Pritchard was ever accused of fraudulent dealings. He was, after all, much too intelligent for that.

With exams due on the sixth week of the course, cramming occupied everyone. I usually tried to escape after tea to find a quiet spot where I could revise. One such spot was in the public gardens where I could spread my books and get my feet up along the seat. Unfortunately, a seedy looking character of about thirty came along and decided he wanted to sit where my feet were. I was annoyed because there were numerous empty seats nearby and he did not have to choose mine. Anyway, I grounded my feet to let him sit down and then returned to my books. He was not to be put off, however, and he started making conversational overtures. It was not until he put his hand on my knee and asked if I would like to have a good time that I lost my rag. I threatened to heave him over the edge if he didn't sod off, and he took the hint.

The exams were not so awful in the event and even Navigation was all right. The great news of the moment, however, was that they would be followed by a three-day leave and I wrote to say that I would be home on the following Friday evening. The course had been tough, tougher physically than mentally, but having survived it and to cap it with leave - even if only for three days - nearly sent me into orbit!

I felt too smugly proud of myself for words as the family greeted me off the London train. My freshly blancoed flash gleamed in my cap and my tunic buttons were shining like white metal. They all made a great fuss of me, Mum looking hard to see behind my eyes, Dad blinking the tears from his and Joan doing her best not to cry. It was not just the uniform though. I guess we all looked a bit different to each other now. The arrow of time was not reversible.

The family left Joan and me alone in the front room for much of the weekend, calling us out occasionally for food. It all passed so quickly though and there was so much to talk about. No sooner had we all met at the station it seemed and they were all seeing me off again. Just to add to my misery I missed the train at Paddington and that was in spite of an extravagant half-a-crown taxi dash from Victoria. I caught the next one, the 6.30 which did not get in to Paignton until 3.00 am, three hours after my pass expired. The guard Sergeant simply told me to "Bugger off" and I heard no more about it.

This was now the seventh week at ITW with the course finished and a posting anxiously awaited. My frustrations were clearly expressed in a letter I wrote to Joan. "Paignton bores me silly now that the course has finished. I put my propellers up on Tuesday - LAC Berry, Leading Aircraftsman that is, equivalent to a Lance Corporal in the army. Rank, isn't it? It does mean 5/6p a day though, plus another 2/- when I start flying!"

But no posting came. Another week passed and still no news from Training Command. The staff was hard put to know what to do with us. After a series of supplementary lectures, organised games were introduced, Flight versus Flight and these were much more acceptable as a fill-in than the extra drills and PT. But everyone, including the staff, was getting extremely bored.

The weather was changing noticeably, not yet cold but distinctly autumnal. Paignton itself appeared to join in the mood of gloom, beginning to look deserted as the holidaymakers departed. I remember wearing my greatcoat for the first time on guard duty and was thankful for it too, as I was for the hot cocoa and beef sandwiches - the big 'perk' of the duty.

Then at long last the postings were listed on Daily Routine Orders - DROs. Three of us from the Flight were posted to No7 Elementary Flying Training School, RAF Desford. The next thing was to find out where Desford was. Someone produced a road map and we found it just outside Leicester, in the Midlands. Beyond that no one had a clue about the place.

We were due to leave the following Monday 22 September. In the event the posting was delayed for yet another week and we did not leave until the 30 September 1941.

CHAPTER 4

The family in Sittingbourne were not only worried about me, but they were also concerned about my sister Vie and young Michael, now living alone in Bearsted with Ron away in the RAF. Vie, unlike Rene, was always thought of as the sensitive and timid one of the two. With her jet-black hair and wide dark eyes she was stunningly beautiful and she had the figure to match. She gave me a book of Wordsworth's poems for my seventeenth birthday, which said more about her than it did me. The fact that I treasured the gift way beyond its intrinsic value also said something, I guess, about our relationship within the family circle. We had an unexpressed empathy with each other, which neither of us ever stopped to examine. We each of us understood the other's sensitivities and inwardness, probably because they contrasted so sharply with the personalities of the other two, Vic and Rene. While Rene would be making a new dress, 20's mini-skirt style no doubt, belted and hip low, Vie would be painting one of her delicate watercolours.

She fell desperately in love at 17, an affair which lasted a year or two and ended with her being jilted. Perhaps she never really got over it, although she subsequently met Ron, her husband-to-be, and thereafter found a secure and loving marriage.

She always seemed to be terribly dominated by Ron who, as far as we could see, ran her life. Their visits to the family up in town felt more like duty calls rather than prompted out of affection. Quite early in the evening (for we Berrys that is) Ron would look at his watch and say, "Come on Vie, it's 10 o'clock. Time we left" and he would round her up and shoo her along like a dog herding sheep. Vie would pause at the door behind Ron's back to grimace and mouth "Isn't he awful!"

Perhaps we never did know the real truth of their relationship, whether she really was as compliant as she always seemed to be, never that is until after her death when it all changed and we saw a completely different Ron, a gentle, thoughtful and most kindly soul. Perhaps he had spent his life protecting this vulnerable woman from the vicissitudes of the world and that she had by some amazing inversion used him mercilessly in the process. We shall never know.

Now, however, the family were worried about her being alone with a young child in a remote Kent village at this time of war. There were air raid alerts most nights and while they were not directed at Bearsted, or Maidstone even, bombs had been dropped nearby. Detling aerodrome, flying off its Spitfires, was after all only a few miles up the road. Mother worried constantly about them. Michael was four years old and without his father around he was already becoming quite a handful and Vie did seem to spoil him somewhat.

Rene, the complete antithesis of Vie, an auburn-haired bustling organiser, finally decided that they had to come and live with them in Sittingbourne. Picking her time carefully, just as Ernest was going on about the cost of the housekeeping, she announced her suggestion that Vie and Mike should come and stay with them.

"She will obviously pay her way - food, light, heating and so on. It would help out with the housekeeping in fact." It was a shrewd argument and one which tipped the scales with Ernest. Any other argument would have produced a dozen reasons against the suggestion. So, Vie and Michael arrived at Ryeburn with numerous suitcases to sit out the war and Ernest was seen to be making good his promise to his partner. They would undoubtedly have been safer to stay in Bearsted which was not under the Luftwaffe flight path to London, but having the support of the family around them was deemed to be worth the extra risks involved.

And that there was a risk was demonstrated the very day after they arrived. I was upstairs when I heard an aeroplane flying very low. Looking out of the window in the direction of London, I saw the grey shape of a large aircraft flying down the road towards the house. I could see quite clearly the black crosses on the underside of the wings. It was a Heinkel 111 and even as I looked I saw the bomb doors open and three objects tumble out. I was downstairs in front of Mum, my mouth opening, when the bombs landed. We saw the clouds of black smoke rising from just behind the High Street a few hundred yards down the road. As an example of opportunity bombing it was very impressive. The pilot had obviously selected the Paper Mills, the only industrial building in an otherwise residential area. Fortunately it had happened on a Sunday when Dad and Vic were at home, otherwise it would have been a bit too close for comfort, their shop virtually backing on to the Mills.

For the first few weeks, Vie and Michael were perfectly happy living with the Pritchards. They had their own room, but ate with Ern, Rene and Beryl. Ron too was very pleased with the arrangement and he wrote warmly to Ern to thank him. Beryl, who was a year older than Michael, played with him blissfully all day long, which was a great relief to everyone. She bossed him remorselessly and Michael thoroughly enjoyed it. A very attractive child, if a rather sly one, she could twist her father around her little finger - the only person in the entire world with such authority.

Inevitably though, minor frictions developed, usually over some misdemeanour of Michael's which Ernest thought that Vie should deal with more firmly than she did. Michael was a naughty child and he did take advantage of his indulgent mother. She would plead with him to be good and he would simply ignore her and push his behaviour as far as he dare. It could be over the dinner table, say, when Michael would demand more of some rationed item and Vie would offer him her portion ...

"Don't give in to the child like that. You just encourage him to be greedy." Ernest's exasperation was understandable but it always caught Vie on a raw nerve. She knew he was right but she felt so vulnerable.

Michael, his face scarlet with anger, would kick his mother under the table. "I want it," he would hiss. And she would give it to him. Ernest would then start a long harangue and Vie would go upstairs crying and Rene would snort and clear the table and Ernest would know that she would not speak to him for days and Beryl would ask him if she could have his butter!

Obviously, things could not go on for long like this and inevitably there was a blazing row over something quite trivial. Ernest told Vie to pack up and get out and Rene, who was by now very demoralised by the weeks of argument, did nothing to intervene. So Vie packed her bags once more and took Michael back to Bearsted. Ron got compassionate leave and dashed home, furious with "that bastard - I could kill him" and moved Vie and Michael into a small furnished house near Maidstone, where they were close to shops, other people and no longer isolated as they had been in Bearsted.

No one really blamed Ernest for throwing Vie out. "It was inevitable. Bound to happen in the end," Dad had said. But no one felt happy about it either. Somehow, because it was Ernest who had done it and it was therefore entirely in character, he got away with it. It was some years later, after the war in fact, before Ron was able to speak again to Ernest and to patch up the quarrel. He only did it then, I guess, out of concern for Vie and the family.

CHAPTER 5

The train from Paignton arrived in Leicester late afternoon. I had travelled up with my two companions, reading and snoozing most of the way, but as we approached Leicester we all roused and began to wipe the steam off the windows to see where we were. None of us knew what Desford would be like in terms of accommodation, food, bull, and service life generally. All we knew was that it was an aerodrome, the first one that any of us had seen after two and a half months in the Air Force. We all felt like old sweats now though, with our Leading Aircraftsman 'props' on our sleeves. No longer were we mere 'Erks', the lowest of the low and with our new status we could even tell Erks to get up off their knees! It was a pleasant feeling - not for being able to order Erks around, that was only theoretical - but to have acquired some status, no matter how insignificant, in a service for which we still had considerable awe.

When we got off the train at Leicester we looked for the RTO (Railway Transport Officer) and he, astonishingly, apparently expected us because he said that transport was on its way. This boosted our egos even further - our station was actually sending transport out to pick us up. Our delight was complete when a large military bus duly arrived, driven by an extremely attractive-looking female in a drab green uniform which none of us could identify but which we all enthusiastically admired.

The drive out to Desford took about half an hour and it was quite dark by the time we arrived. We could see damn all of the place except for the outline of the building in front of which we had parked. Our driver shepherded us through a blackout lobby and along a corridor to a door marked **ADMINISTRATION**. We were greeted by the inevitable corporal who laboriously wrote our rank, names and time into a scruffy ledger on which was the large label **BOOK IN**. We then returned to the bus to collect our kit-bags and the corporal led us towards what in the darkness looked like a group of single storey huts.

"This is your hut, No 4. Remember where it is so that you can find it again. It's a big airfield out there, and you could spend the night under a hedge." He nodded gloomily over his shoulder.

Inside the hut and with the door shut and the light on, we were at the end of a long corridor with six doors off either side. The corporal stopped at the second door. "This is your room, Berry." He unlocked the door and I looked in to what might have been a bedroom in any two star hotel. A divan bed was made up with freshly laundered sheets and dark brown blankets, a bedside cabinet was complete with a table lamp and in the corner was a white porcelain lavatory basin beneath a large wall mirror. Thick curtains hung at the window and a rug covered most of the floor.

"I'm sorry I haven't a room with a bath, but you're a bit late arriving." I looked round sharply at him, almost believing what he was saying. Anything would have been possible at that moment.

"It is pretty good isn't it? You're a lucky lot of buggers, you cadets. You even have an Erk who cleans and makes your bed up every day."

"I don't believe it." I stared at him hard, but he was speaking the truth. The cadets really did have a marvellous time at Desford compared with what many other aspiring pilots must have suffered elsewhere. For the moment, the realities of life at EFTS were exceeding our wildest imaginings.

"All this, *and* two bob a day flying pay?" I shook my head in stupefying amazement. "Where's the catch?" "Ah. The catch is when you wash out flying and remuster back into the Airforce, with the rest of us in the 'Mob'." The corporal glared at us, turned and went out into the corridor. "Come on. I'll show you the mess. Perhaps the grub will bring you back to Earth."

After groping behind the corporal in the darkness for a while our eyes began to accustom to the night. There was the beginning of a new moon, the thinnest crescent imaginable, and I could just make out the massive shape of a large hangar on the right of us. The next building, also on the right, a few minutes later was identified by the corporal as the Officers' Mess. This building appeared to be on a corner, for the road went round it at right angles, as far as I could tell, and there appeared to be nothing beyond it, no buildings, no hedges, nothing. The corporal said, "That's the airfield!"

Walking at night in the country was a peculiar sensation for a 'townie' like me. I had never before experienced such total darkness. The void that was the airfield in the night was wholly unexpected. The vast open space out there felt tangible, real. I remember shivering and not because of the crisp autumnal air. It felt wet with a heavy dew and I felt absurdly relieved when we reached the friendly shape of another building. This time it was on our left and away from the airfield. We fumbled our way through a pair of Crittal-glazed doors, fighting the inevitable blackout curtains and arrived in the entrance lobby of the Mess. The corporal told us that the doors through the left hand side of the lobby led to the Sergeants' Mess, a holier than holy place, never to be broached, not even on the pain of death. Our Mess, the Airmen's Mess, was on the right.

The evening meal had long since been finished, but amazingly, sandwiches had been left for our anticipated late arrival - spam sandwiches and strong, stewed cocoa, both immensely welcome.

When I walked out from the hut the next morning I could identify the buildings we had groped around in darkness the previous night. The huts themselves I could now see were solidly built, rendered externally and with low-pitched roofs. Opposite on the other side of the access road were two enormous hangars and in the gap in between them a two-storey building, again rendered, with a square tower rising from one corner. This I later discovered was the Aerodrome Control Tower. To the right of the huts was a further large, two-storey, rendered and flat roofed building, which was to become very familiar later to us as the Ground Instruction Block.

In peacetime all these buildings had gleamed brilliantly like white Corbusien chalets on the Mediterranean, but now they were all heavily camouflaged in drab green and brown and black. The style of the architecture was 1930's 'moderne' rather than 1930's Bauhaus 'modern', that is with naive symmetries and not the self-conscious asymmetries of the real thing - all very art deco and à la Crittal.

Further down the road where it continued past the large hangars, was the Officers' Mess, again a rendered and flat roofed symmetrical building with an Odeonesque tower feature. On the opposite corner was a group of very functional and temporary-looking huts, black bitumastic felt-clad arrangements which housed diverse activities such as the armoury, the Sick Bay and the toy known as the Link Trainer.

The Sergeants' and Airmen's' Mess building was similar to that of the Officers' Mess, apart from the tower feature, and it too was painted out with the same drab camouflage. The whole environment however, in the hazy October sun looked trim and well organised, like a model village. My first impressions were highly favourable.

"There doesn't seem to be much bullshit about the place either," I said as we walked over to the GI Block.

We joined dozens of others, like ourselves newly arrived, in a large lecture hall and contributed to the buzz of excited speculation which died immediately a Squadron Leader stepped on to the platform in front of us.

"My name is John Wardell and I am the Chief Flying Instructor. Welcome to Desford."

We listened intently, hanging on to every lilting Irish syllable. He was a large man, large in frame, large in personality and with large expansive gestures. He told us how we would be allocated to Flights, how we would alternate mornings and afternoons between flying and lectures plus other activities such as the Link Trainer, gunnery, organised games and so on.

"At the end of the course, which will encompass from thirtyfive to fifty hours flying, including night flying, you will be posted to your Service Flying Training Station, where you will fly Masters, or twin-engined Oxfords or Ansons, depending on whether you are to become fighter or bomber pilots."

If a poll had been taken at that minute as to what everyone wanted the result would have been a unanimous vote for the Masters.

The figure on the platform epitomised the ideal of these still very idealistic young men, with his dark wavy hair, the enthusiasm and above all, the brevet and medal ribbons on his chest. The same scene on a training airfield in Germany would have looked like contrived propaganda, but here it was simple naive enthusiasm.

Chief Flying Instructor Squadron Leader Wardell AFC addressing cadet pilots, RAF Desford, 1941
Photograph courtesy of the Imperial War Museum, London

The speakers who followed the CFI could not maintain the same excitement, although the Chief Ground Instructor, Flight Lieutenant Hill, did evoke a sense of awe with his patched and mended face, all burn-scar tissue, from an early flying accident.

We cadets were told to report to the stores at 1400 hours to collect our flying kit. This gave us time to wander across the road and to peer in between the hangars at the airfield. It looked vast and empty. It was quite a shock, this first experience of an airfield, the wide flat open space found nowhere else in man-made environments in the UK. There were no trees for miles, no buildings, no hedges even, just flat grass to the horizon.

On the very edges of the field however, we could see four low blister hangars each with half a dozen or so Tiger Moths parked nearby like small insects. These were the flight dispersals we had been told about earlier. I confess to feeling my heartbeat increasing slightly as I faced into the stiff southwesterly breeze. In front of the first hangar a windsock kicked and flicked noisily, sometimes over the horizontal. It was very exhilarating, like facing a strong sea breeze. Even the Tigers were rocking fretfully on their pickets.

We had little idea what to expect at the kitting-out parade and the reality was no anti-climax. We first drew an all-enveloping, waterproof flying suit called a Sidcot. One stepped into this, then zipped it up to the neck and down the legs and arms. It had a high fur collar and numerous pockets on the chest and knees. If this were not enough to keep out the cold we were also given an inner suit, a dark brown cotton padded affair which also zipped up to the neck and down the arms and legs.

A Cadet Pilot wearing a Sidcot flying suit with early issue flying boots
Photograph courtesy of the Imperial War Museum, London

Next came the leather helmet with its round bun-like earpieces which unzipped to take the earphones and their plastic covers. In place of earphones however, we had what were called Gosport Tubes - a device like a doctor's stethoscope - a communication hangover from much earlier days of flying.

The goggles were complicated affairs with metal-hinged frames and padded leather designed to fit closely to the face. I was next equipped with a beautiful pair of suede leather fur-lined flying boots which zipped up to just below the knees. The gloves too were superior leather gauntlets, in addition to which we were issued a pair of silk inner gloves. "Flying is going to be a cold business by the look of it," someone said.

Finally we drew a set of maps and a quarto size notebook. This last item was really the only disappointment. We were told that it was to serve as our Pilot's Flying Log Book and that we would have to rule it up accordingly. "It saves the expense of wasting a real Log Book when you are washed out," was the laconic explanation from the Erk in the stores. All this kit involved yet another kitbag in which to carry it.

First log book

The highlight of the next day, Thursday 2nd October, was the visit to the Parachute Section. It was located in the first hangar, a long high-ceilinged room down the centre of which ran an immense polished table. The parachutes were in racks either side of the room with a number open and hanging from the ceiling at the end of the room. One of the cadets was required to put on a parachute and this was then adjusted to fit so tightly that he was doubled over and barely able to walk. We were told that if the harness was at all loose, the two straps between the legs were as effective a castration device as you could ever get!

The parachute wallah then pulled the ripcord and showed how the small pilot chute deployed with its springs to pull the main chute out of the pack. He told us that every chute is periodically opened like this and hung to dry in the heated atmosphere of the Section to ensure they are in prime condition when really needed. We were then initiated into the art of parachute folding and packing on the long polished table - an amazing skill, to fold so much silk into such a small space.

The whole exercise should have given every cadet supreme confidence in his parachute. That was the idea. However, there were some of us there who lost whatever faith they previously had and to whom the device looked so Heath Robinson!

"I wonder how many pairs of knickers it would make?" was another line of thought.

Cadets collecting their parachutes
Photograph courtesy of the Imperial War Museum, London

CHAPTER 6

Horace Berry, my father, missed his motorcar. He had sold it, or at least Ernest had persuaded him to part with it when he first got down to Sittingbourne.

"You can't afford to run it, man, and fifty quid in your pocket would be very useful to you now."

Then there was petrol rationing and he could not go far on it anyway. But it was worth a lot more than fifty pounds, he thought. In the end he did let his son-in-law have it, as he did need the money. Now, with the shop bringing in enough to get them by, he regretted selling. It rankled too when he saw it marked up at £149 in the showroom. He never did tell his wife that. Why stir up bad feeling? Dad was always one for a quiet life.

He had been mobile ever since the days of BB Engineering - BB for Berry and Bush - the Engineering works he opened in the early 1920's on the corner of Jarvis Road in Dulwich. There were double shop premises on the front, trading in motorcycles, bicycles, petrol, wirelesses, electrical goods and every conceivable accessory one could think of. At the rear were quite extensive engineering shops capable of undertaking most engineering fabrications of the time. This was in the twenties and thirties and I remember as a very young child the awesome chugging gas engine, protected by a waist-high brass rail, in the back of the rearmost shop. It throbbed and spun in the gloom, driving the endless, slapping, overhead leather belt which gave power to the various lathes as well as the generator. The works were lit from the generator and the lights went up and down in time with the slow rhythm of the gas engine. In one corner was another infernal machine, a coke brazier, powered by foot-operated bellows. I can see my father now, standing over the dish of white-hot coke, his goggles sparkling in their reflected glow, with the gas torch in one hand blasting a tongue of fire and the other manipulating the brazing rod in the furnace. In memory it was as near a scene from Dante's Inferno as I could imagine.

Dad had an AJS motor bike, then a water-cooled Scott - a tremendous innovation for its time - although this was exchanged later for a 350 BSA with sidecar which transported the young family to places like Eastbourne for our annual holiday.

The cycle shop in Sittingbourne was never going to make enough for him to buy another car and it was then that he saw the GPO advert in the paper for postmen. The money was quite good. He thought about it - a regular steady job, not too arduous. The thought of being employed, when he had been self-employed all his life, was quite a novelty. Security of employment, that's what they talked about.

"What do you think, Hetty? Shall I apply?" My mother just glared at him. She had no need to say anything. But for once Dad did what he wanted to do.

Apart from his aching feet sometimes and the early morning starts, he actually enjoyed the work. He enjoyed the companionship of the other men in the sorting office, the level of humour and the general ribbing which went on constantly. And above all he enjoyed that great mug of steaming hot tea when he got home. Rene said nothing but she was a bit worried by how grey his face looked these days. The October mornings could be quite cold.

Dad bought an old Morris Minor from Ernie. He gave him £85 for it and it was nowhere near as good as his old car either. But he and mother enjoyed it. They took Vic, Doreen and young Peter down to Margate that Sunday. It was quite a squeeze for all five of them, but the weather was bright and fresh and not cold really for the time of year, and Peter loved it.

They sat on the sand and ate their lunch while Peter built a brave, moated castle, decorated with black and white shells. Then the tide lapped in and filled the moat and slowly eroded the castle and it dissolved and returned to the wet sand. After that it really got too chilly to stay on the beach much longer and they retreated to a teashop where they could sit and still look out to sea. Peter was obviously tired by now and getting fractious. "He's been very good really, Mum, but he has been up a long time."

"And what about you, young lady?" And Mum looked down at Doreen's now visibly bulging waistline. "You don't want to overdo things now do you?"

"Oh, I'm alright." She fluttered her hands dismissively, and then rearranged the cups and saucers on the table, still desperately unsure of herself - just as she was when she was only seventeen.

Vic, unusually sensitive to his wife's unease, stood up. "Come on, we should be moving. Let's get my family home." Which immediately set Peter off grizzling about wanting to go on the beach again. "Why do good things always have to end in tears?" Mum asked as she picked up her bag and moved towards the door. It had been a good day too. The air raid sirens went off just as they got home.

I had to report to my flight dispersal at 0900 - D Flight - halfway around the perimeter, having first collected my parachute from the Section on the hangar apron. What with the parachute and the flying gear, I was sweating by the time I had reached the dispersal, although the morning was quite chilly.

My companion was older than me, about 25 I guessed, a schoolmasterish sort of person with a Stalinesque moustache. I wrote home saying what a decent type George Thame was. We had chummed up the first evening in the mess and seemed to fall naturally into each other's company. George was very confident and organised and it helped me to have him around, for I felt just a wee bit apprehensive although I would never have admitted it. There was a lot of banter about box kites, string and sealing wax, flying prams and 'don't forget to tighten your jock straps', which hardly helped the nervous.

The Dispersal Hut was primitive, furnished with an assortment of collapsible, collapsing and collapsed chairs, rickety trestle tables, lockers, aircraft recognition pin-ups and a large blackboard. Heating, when it was on that is, was from a freestanding, cast iron stove in the middle of the floor.

The hut was divided basically into two, with we cadets in one half and the instructors and the Flight Commander's office in the other. The first thing one noticed was the blackboard. It listed the names of six flying instructors with the names of two cadets against each instructor. I saw that I was allocated to a Pilot Officer Tillet.

There were a couple of young civilian lads sitting on chairs outside the hut who ignored us totally as we arrived and a third lad who had been in deep conversation with a rather plump girl of about twenty. We heard a "Morning Sir" chorus in broad Leicestershire accents from these lads and a very casual looking Flight Lieutenant came in the door. We cadets all sprang to attention which seemed to surprise the officer.

"Good morning. Er...Carry on," and he disappeared into the instructors' room. He reappeared a few minutes later to introduce himself as the Flight Commander, Flight Lieutenant Wynne-Powell, and told us that our flying instructors would be calling us out individually as per the names on the board.

"You can store your flying gear in the lockers and sign for the keys from Audrey. She's the blonde job who books you in and out on your flights as well. Remember, incidentally, you never, *repeat never*, go flying solo without first booking out and signing the form 700." He looked around the hut with a pained expression.

"And for Christ's sake try to keep the place a bit tidy. It's like a bloody pigsty."

There were parachutes and flying gear stacked and piled everywhere and the place did look a shambles. But then it always had and no doubt it always would and the Flight Commander would continue to moan about it, as he always did!

One by one the instructors came in and called for their pupils. Pilot Officer Tillet was very tall, fair-haired, in his mid-twenties and with a very public school clipped voice. I must say that I did not feel any immediate rapport. The instructor took me and his other pupil out to one of the Tiger Moths.

"The De Havilland 82a, the RAF ab initio trainer with a 130 horse power Gypsy Major engine. This is a very easy aeroplane to fly, but one of the hardest to fly well! Let's walk around it and name the parts, as it were."

He identified, over-obviously I thought, the ailerons, the wing-slots and the rudder and elevators. The petrol tank sat in between the top wings with a primitive glass float to indicate the fuel level. It held 18 gallons he said. "Enough for two and a half hours flying. And this is the Pitot Tube, a venturi device which registers your speed through the air on the airspeed indicator in the cockpit."

I took these explanations with a mixture of keen interest tempered by a sense of irritation at some of the talking-down the officer lapsed into. Both me and Bob Eaves, the other cadet, however, were astonished by the apparent frailty and primitive nature of the aircraft. For example, there was a metal quadrant fixed to one of the wing struts from the top of which hinged a sort of pendulum and when the aircraft was climbing the pendulum would stay vertical thus indicating the angle of climb against the quadrant. It was unbelievable in the context of modern aviation and warfare. Another surprise was when the instructor told us the aeroplane had no brakes.

"The only thing stopping you when you land, or taxi, is the tail skid. The Tiger doesn't have a tail wheel and you have to rely upon the friction of that thing over the grass to slow you down. Remember that when you are taxiing! Now let's have a look in the office." PO Tillet climbed up on to the left wing where there was a tread strip on its surface and had we two pupils either side of the rear cockpit, where two flaps hinged down to give access.

"Now, going from left to right, we start with the throttle, back for closed and forwards for open. This second lever is the mixture control. The mixture is already set so you must never use that lever. Oh yes, that's the throttle nut which you must tighten before take off, otherwise the throttle vibrates closed and you're up the creek! Underneath there you have the petrol tap, and the two pedals on which you put your feet are the rudder bar. That, of course, is the joy stick," and he waggled it around in a three hundred and sixty degree circle. "Over on the right there is the lock for the wing slots and down here by the side of the seat is the tail trimmer."

He next went round the instrument dash with its blind-flying panel and the gimbal-mounted compass, finishing with the two magneto switches on the fuselage by the windscreen. "Two switches because there are two sets of ignition to give you a back-up in case one of them fails."

We walked back to the flight hut, PO Tillet always half a step in front of us no matter how hard we tried to keep up with him. He seemed to be impelled by a lot of nervous energy.

"OK Berry, get your gear on and we'll go for a flight."

Before the RAF moved in, Desford was a civilian airfield owned by Reid and Sigrist Limited, the aircraft instrument manufacturers. Reid and Sigrist, in fact, were still on the airfield in hangars on the south side and away from the RAF who occupied everywhere and everything else. Major Reid, a large rubicund and tweedy gentleman, was to be seen occasionally in the Officers' Mess, no doubt keeping an eye on his investment and being dined by the Commanding Officer, Wing Commander John Beaumont.

Alex Henshaw and the Snargasher, RAF Desford, 1941
Photograph courtesy of the Imperial War Museum, London

Quite early in the war, production of the Spitfire was dispersed from the giant Supermarine factory at Castle Bromwich to the four satellites at Cosford, Cowley, Sywell and Desford and it was commonplace to see a Spitfire weaving through the clouds of Tiger Moths above these airfields.

As I struggled out to the aeroplane, parachute over my shoulder, I heard something much noisier than a Gypsy Major engine behind me. I turned and there, just above the dispersal, was a Spitfire droning in - but inverted. Even as I looked I saw its wheels go up as if it intended to land. It clattered massively overhead, hanging from the sky, and then when it seemed to be only twelve feet or so up, it casually rolled over and landed perfectly.

After I was strapped into my seat and with my Gosport plugged in, PO Tillet's voice came through. "That was Alex Henshaw, Chief Test Pilot for Supermarine. He doesn't usually get in our way, but he does like to show off a bit."

CHAPTER 7

I left school at the age of 14 without much hope of an academic career. My health had been awful for most of my school days, with chronic bronchial asthma following a bout of whooping cough when I was three. I would attend school for two weeks and then spend two weeks in bed. Perhaps I had been kept off school too much by an over-protective mother, but it would have made little difference had I been able to attend more often. The teaching was always too fractured for me to make much sense of it, although I did amaze my maths teacher on one occasion. My attendance pattern fortuitously allowed me to catch the introduction of a new mathematical concept to the class and when they came to work an example, I was the only lad out of thirty who showed that I had understood it. My teacher, the formidable and much feared Mr Rouseau, treated me thereafter much more thoughtfully, almost with respect. Word must have got around the staff room too, because the science master, Mr Hollis, began to give me individual attention and even made me a sort of technician, helping the other lads with their bench work and staying behind during break to set up the experiments.

I read insatiably. There was a second-hand bookshop on the parade and I used to buy one or more books a week, usually in the Collins Pocket Classics series, at 3d each. I got through many of the popular titles by the obvious authors such as Charles Kingsley, Walter Scott, Lord Lytton, Dickens, Fenimore Cooper, Mark Twain, Tolstoy and of course Conan Doyle, Wells, Jules Verne, John Buchan and even Richmal Crompton! They were an eclectic group, but my favourite by far was Alexandre Dumas and I devoured everything I could find of his, The Three Musketeers, 20 Years After, The Vicomte De Bragalonne, The Fencing Master, The Black Tulip, The Chevalier De Maison Rouge, Chicot the Jester and so on. My worst book was George Elliot's Adam Bede, The only book I have never been able to finish. I wonder what that says about me? I still have them all, even now, fifty years on, faded, tatty, yellow and falling apart, but they were my magic mirror upon a dream world.

I told the careers master that I wanted to be an architect and so, when I left school, they got me a job in an estate agency. It was a good try really and they had done their best for me. Unfortunately, and as a very small step on the way to becoming an architect, it was not very helpful. The office was that of a closed agency and its work the management of a housing estate in Nunhead. There was only me and my boss Mr Thompson in the office, although we were assisted on the first few days of every month by a Mrs Castle who, it transpired, was Mr Thompson's sister. The first of the month was rent day for the thousand or so tenants involved. The rest of the time between collecting rents was spent logging tenants' complaints about broken sash cords and taps that needed new washers and the like.

The office was divided down the middle by an elbow-high mahogany counter. Mr Thompson's desk was at one end near the window and mine was at the other end. Mr Thompson had a glass front to his desk behind which he would snooze after lunch. Mine was open to the public. There was an old gas fire behind the counter, which hissed soporifically and after lunch it sometimes had me nodding off as well. I had to keep the cast iron tray in front of it topped up with water to prevent the awful throbbing headache I would get by the end of the afternoon. The back room was filled with racks of wallpaper and one of my jobs was to help the tenants to select the wallpaper for the redecoration of their houses, which was done on a strict rota. I got so depressed with the tedium of handling these rolls of paper for the 'dithering old biddies' that I eventually made up pattern books of the range of papers available and then I only had to note their choice and bundle up the necessary rolls for the decorator when he called.

The boredom of the day was relieved by visits from Tom, the Yard Foreman. Tom was a rough one, not one of "yer orffice types what don't know the diff'rence between a 'ammer and a mallet." He would stand rolling a shapeless cigarette in his grubby fingers, sniffing along the back of his hand, and chewing his gums as he told me about how the plumber had scored with Mrs Brown up Athenlay Road. Not that I approved of such stories, but Tom liked me, I believe, "You don't think you was Christ Almighty all the time" he would say with a nod towards the window desk. It was fine until Mr Thompson or Mrs Castle came in and then Tom would become all business-like and start knuckling his forehead and shuffling his clay-heavy boots out across the polished lino.

The head office of the Estate was up in London and every morning old Mr Lenny, who lived on the estate, would come in to collect the previous day's rents to take up to head office. It was a ritual peppered by years of resentment on one side and smugness on the other. Mr Lenny, dry, grey, acerbic and faintly superior, would count the money, put it away in his old leather attaché case, along with his copy of the Times, and then sit back to discuss the day's news. Mr Thompson, his heavy jowls bobbing, would shuffle the papers on his desk as if too busy for such trivia, but Mr Lenny, oblivious to such ploys, would insist upon the proper notice being taken of his wisdom before sweeping grandly out of the office with always the same smug "See you tomorrow." Why on earth the money was not banked locally instead of wasting everyone's time in this way was totally inexplicable to me.

The enormous event in my life at this time however, was a young girl by the name of Marie Roche. I can barely write the name now without going off into some misty daydream. She was only fourteen when I first met her; I was a year older than she and it was the start of a deep and passionate love-affair, one which I probably never fully got over for the rest of my life. There were only the two of us - no gang of kids hanging around and perhaps this was why it all got so intense and serious. We used to meet after tea at seven o'clock most evenings and walk hand in hand along Brenchley Gardens, up Sydenham Hill and sometimes as far as Sydenham Wells Park, before turning back. Then, if there was time - and there usually was - we would turn into the unlit cutting behind Horniman Gardens to make love.

I was a very properly brought up young man in accordance with the almost puritanical standards of the time and nothing in the world, other than Marie herself perhaps, would have induced me to overstep the mark in my relationship with this young girl. I loved and deeply respected her and our passions would rise to white heat and in my case sometimes beyond, leaving me both uncomfortable and ashamed. When St Peter's clock struck ten she would kiss me tenderly, button her blouse and drag us both away.

The amazing thing was that while my family knew of our relationship, Marie insisted upon it being kept secret from her family and seemingly, for the two or so years that it lasted, they never did know. How she could go in, night after night, her freckled cheeks scarlet, her blond hair dishevelled, slightly distrait and without her parents questioning where she had been, and with whom, was something I could never understand.

It all began to go wrong when Marie was evacuated with her school at the outbreak of war. I cycled the twenty-plus miles to Redhill a few times to see her, but these trips were more painful than pleasurable. To me, in my misery at our separation, she seemed too happy and full of all the exciting things that were happening. I began to suspect she had found another beau.

The evacuation did not last long, however, and when the expected air raids never happened the kids began to drift back to London. Marie's school returned, but the regular pattern of our evenings together failed to resume somehow, although at first I did wait for her at our usual meeting place. Then, just before Christmas and after a couple of weeks of not seeing each other, she put a note through my door asking me to meet her. At last, it all seemed to be back to normal, with her snuggling closely up to me and saying how much she had missed me and how she really could not go on without me. She pleased me particularly by asking me to try on a woollen glove, one of a pair she said she was knitting me for Christmas.

We arranged to meet the following evening, but she never turned up.

I never heard from her again although I saw her quite often, once with her mother, when she walked right passed me her eyes resolutely fixed straight ahead. Such meetings were agonising, I was still desperately in love with her, but too proud to pursue her in any way. If she wanted me, she would now have to make the first move.

She did seem to make a few signals thereafter which I resolutely ignored. She would cycle round and round in the road by the house at the time I would be due home, but I would ignore her. I really felt too hurt to risk any more. In retrospect I reasoned that I had probably suffocated the girl with my enveloping passion and that I had finally scared her away. We were both far too young to get so serious and she had run frightened in spite of whatever she might have felt for me. I had only myself to blame.

I was a very lonely and heart-forlorn lad who moped through that first year of war although I did try very hard to find another girl. I fell in with a local group who included a young brunette called Helen. She was demonstrably in love with me, but she failed miserably to catch my interest. Gwyneth, slightly older and very much the leader of the group, did her best to pair us off, having read poor Helen's desperation. She would leave us with some fatuous excuse on Horniman Drive, leaning against the wall of one of the new houses then under construction, Helen's head on my shoulder, as we looked out over London at the setting sun. But nothing ever came of it. Poor Helen, she hadn't a hope with Marie's ghost still lingering.

CHAPTER 8

I felt half suffocated by the Sutton Harness straps. I could barely move a muscle, nor breathe it seemed, where the prop-swinger had lashed me in so tightly. I was sweating profusely inside all the flying gear from my exertions. The prop-swinger was standing in front of the aeroplane, his left hand casually up on the prop blade.

"Switches off, petrol on, sucking in, Mr Tillet." I saw Tillet's hand go up over the switches. "Switches off, petrol on."

The prop-swinger began to rotate the large propeller which kicked over compression viciously. He did this three times and then, "Contact?"

I felt and saw the control column jerk back into my stomach, the throttle advance about a quarter and heard Tillet's response. "Contact!"

The prop-swinger heaved the blade down, stepping backwards as his hand followed through. There was a great burst of noise and the propeller disappeared in a swirl of motion, the whole aeroplane vibrated alarmingly and a gale of wind whipped dust and grass past the cockpit. I did not know which was more terrifying, the noise or the vibration. Both got worse however, when Tillet ran the engine up to full throttle. The aeroplane shook as if it would self-destruct and the noise was overwhelming, so that it was an enormous relief when he closed the throttle again. The engine tick-over seemed placid in contrast to the previous cacophony.

There followed much stirring of the control column before Tillet waved his hand across the front of his face and the prop-swinger, who had been stationed at the wing tip, ran in and pulled the chocks away from beneath the wheels. The throttle opened as if self-willed and the Tiger Moth began to trundle forwards. Our progress was erratic with the nose of the aeroplane swinging from side to side which seemed to be necessary in fact to see where we were going because the nose of the aeroplane completely obliterated forward vision. I could see nothing otherwise in the angle of about fifty degrees straight ahead.

The entire aeroplane seemed to resonate with the noise of the tailskid scraping over the turf and the ground undulations beneath the wheels were exaggerated to great dips and heaves at the tips of the wings. My heart was thumping as if to keep pace with the engine. We swept round the perimeter of the airfield and finally came to rest at right angles to the take-off path. I saw the tail trimmer move forward about two-thirds in its quadrant and Tillet's voice came over the Gosport tubes.

"We are ready now to take off. We will climb up to about a thousand feet and just have a gentle cruise around. Are you OK?" I swallowed. I was as ready as I would ever be. "Why the hell did I volunteer?" I thought, and out loud, "Yes Sir." And then again to myself, "Please God, don't let me be sick."

The throttle opened, the Tiger swung slowly round into wind and with the stick right back in my stomach it began to trundle forward. There was a mind-stopping pause and then all hell broke loose - the throttle opened fully and I was pressed back in my seat by acceleration as the aeroplane surged forwards. The noise was again deafening. The stick was now pushed away from me and towards the compass under the dashboard. The clatter and the bouncing and the buffeting were tremendous and lasted for about ten seconds as the aeroplane sped faster and faster. Then the nose seemed to drop - and suddenly - all the noise and vibration stopped. It was a magic moment - we were airborne.

The aeroplane did not seem to climb - the ground fell away and I was amazed at the rapidly changing perspective of the countryside. I had no sense of height, no sense of anticipated vertigo as the aerodrome lowered away beneath me, the hangars looking like models on the landscape. It felt distinctly cold now and the colours of everything seemed to be changing and darkening as we climbed up towards the cloud base.

After a few minutes the engine note reduced to a steady clatter and the nose of the aeroplane dropped down to the horizon.

We were flying level with just occasional dips and wobbles, like going over a humped back bridge at speed. It was not alarming and, suddenly aware of how tense I was, I made an effort to relax and to enjoy this utterly amazing experience. I could see people like little ants and a car going along a road and houses. In a field there was a bonfire burning with a long trail of white smoke pencilled from it. The slipstream buffeted my face when I got too close to the edge of the cockpit and it was icy. The atmosphere up here seemed so cold and damp with streaks of mist whipping past. Straight ahead the horizon was as though drawn with a brush of dark blue where it met the inverted dish of grey cloud above.

Suddenly the world tipped up sideways, my stomach lurched, and the wings pivoted down and around a large clump of trees, the nose sliding along the horizon for a bit before the wings returned to their - thank God - normal position parallel to the horizon. I had barely settled again after the disorientation of the turn, when it all happened again. This time I was half expecting it and it did not seem so bad.

"There's the aerodrome on the left." Tillet's voice startled me. I looked over my shoulder and saw the large clear expanse of the airfield with its toy hangars and other buildings and numerous Tiger Moths scattered over it, some of them moving like crawling flies.

"The cloud base is quite low today. Are you enjoying it?"

My enthusiastic "Yes Sir. Terrific." was genuine. I felt quite secure, with no ball-shrinking reaction at the height and just a wonderful amazement at this unique aerial perspective where everything changed second by second.

"Good. We'll go in and land now." and the aeroplane once more banked to the left, the engine cutting back and the nose dipping down. The sudden deceleration and exaggerated nose down attitude caught me by surprise and I tensed up again. We were gliding across the downwind boundary, getting lower and lower, the noise of the air through the rigging wires drowning that of the throttled-back engine. Then the nose went even lower and we banked round towards the airfield. The last few seconds happened very quickly, the ground rushing up to meet us faster and faster. At the last moment it seemed we checked our descent, flew parallel with the ground for a few moments and then settled down gently on to the grass. Without a vestige of previous experience in such things, I knew that it was a perfect landing.

I joined the other pupils in the dispersal and for the first time in my life I swore - "That was bloody marvellous ... but I don't think I'll ever be able to do it!"

We had all had our first 'air experience' trip and were buzzing each other about it as we stood around the YMCA Tea Van. "Did you see the church in Desford Village?" - "He pushed the stick forward and left my stomach up there somewhere." - "We were doing 85 according to the ASI." - "It was bloody wizard." - "The sky's full of them ... They're like mosquitoes." "Did you see that Spit?" ...

Tillet came over to the van. "If you've finished your tea let's go and learn how to fly." I put my mug up on to the counter and ran back in to the dispersal to collect my helmet and parachute. Someone called out "Good luck," as I shuffled past the group around the van, "I'll need it, mate." under my breath.

After Tillet had signalled for chocks away, he told me to put my left hand on the throttle, my right on the stick and my feet on the pedals.

"You can always do this while we are flying to feel what I am doing. *But do not grip the stick*", he emphasised, "just hold it lightly between your finger and thumb.... Now, to start taxiing hold the stick right back in your stomach and open the throttle slowly. When the aeroplane starts to move, adjust the throttle to maintain this sort of pace."

As we taxied out Tillet explained that the only control one had on the ground was with the throttle and the rudder. "Taxi at a fast walking pace, like this and remember you haven't got any brakes. The only way to stop is by closing the throttle, so keep a strict lookout ahead." He then confirmed my deduction about weaving the nose from side to side. "Very coarse movements on the rudder bar are necessary and remember, never taxi in a straight line. We have more accidents that way than we ever do flying!"

Aeroplanes were taking off and landing all the time and it was necessary to wait on the boundary until there was a clear path across the airfield. Fortunately every one seemed to be taking off and landing more or less in the same direction using the full width of the field, otherwise ... and I shook my head at the thought. There were three windsocks around the perimeter and obviously they were the key to the orderly traffic. But what happens if there is no wind, I wondered?

The take-off and climb were similar to the first trip, only this time I held the stick, albeit timidly, in between my fingers as Tillet had suggested. Once we had levelled out, Tillet's voice came through, "I'm going to show you the effects of the controls" and he demonstrated how moving the stick to the left and right banked the aeroplane, and moving it forwards and backwards lowered and raised the nose. The fore and aft movements left me clutching the sides of the cockpit in sudden panic as the aeroplane lurched over into a dive and then up into a climb.

"OK. I'm convinced." I think I said it to myself.

Slewing the nose left and right with the rudder was almost as disturbing, making me feel as if I was skidding out of the cockpit.

"Now I want you to take over and keep the aeroplane straight and level.... You've got it!" I stiffened, shocked and surprised and tightened my grip on the stick.

"I've got it" and under my breath, "God help us."

It was a revelation. The controls felt so light and the response was immediate and exaggerated. But I think I kept the wings roughly level with the horizon after a bit and the nose thereabouts.

"The nose is wandering to the right all the time. Use the rudder." I concentrated hard. It was like thinking of five different things at the same time. If I got the wings level the nose would drop and if I pulled the nose up the wings would stray.

"Sight something straight ahead on the horizon, like that big clump of trees there and then keep the nose on it with the rudder."

This simplified the problem immediately, but the nose still kept dropping below the horizon.

"I think you must be trimmed a bit nose-heavy. Move the tail trimmer back a notch." I took the stick in my right hand and fumbled down for the tail trimmer. The nose began to gyrate alarmingly and I felt a guiding pressure on the stick as I notched the tail trimmer back. This time the nose stayed put and after a bit so did the wings.

"That's fine," Tillet said, "You're beginning to relax and getting the hang of it." It was quite true, I did feel happier and positively began to enjoy flying this contraption.

"If you look at your turn and bank indicator, you'll see that as soon as the nose wanders with the wings level the top needle skids sideways. You have to keep that needle dead centre with the rudder. OK?"

Tillet took control back and we returned to the airfield and landed. We had been airborne for forty-five minutes and I felt exhausted, but intensely happy.

There was no flying on the next day, Saturday 4th October, and everyone decided it was a good opportunity to explore Leicester. George Thame and a group of the lads planned to catch the bus in from Desford Village at about 3 o'clock, do some shopping, have a meal somewhere and then find a local for some beer. I was invited, but cried off on the grounds that I had to shop and then return to get some letters written. George did his best to persuade me to go along, but I resisted. And that was how it worked out, with me coming home on the bus quite early.

There was no flying in fact for the next two days, which browned everyone off. The cloud base had clamped right down and a fine mist of continuous rain filled the air most of the time reducing visibility to fifty yards or so. But we cadets were quickly scheduled for an alternative torture called the Link Trainer.

The Link was a rather boxy mock-up of a monoplane complete with wings, rudder and elevators. Instead of a conventional undercarriage however, it was balanced on the end of a stout rod rising from a large black box. There was a hood which closed down over the cockpit so that its occupant was then visually isolated. The objective of the Link was to teach and to provide practice in instrument flying.

The instructor sat at a nearby desk, connected by phone with the pupil to whom he would issue instructions about what courses to fly, the height, air speed to maintain and so on. The actual track which the pupil flew was then traced out on paper by a crab for comparison with the course set by the instructor. The engine noise was also simulated to add realism and the link actually banked and tilted fore and aft in response to the controls. An additional refinement to the torture was 'rough air'. When this was switched on, the Link bucked and lurched like a wild horse, making it extremely difficult to maintain a course with the instruments flickering all over the place.

EFTS cadets had to cover a twelve-hour course usually consisting of half-hour lessons two or three times a week. The occasions when flying was washed out were obviously a good time to fit in some Link Trainer practice.

My first experience was enjoyable. The cockpit was fully equipped with flying controls, throttle and compass. The instrument panel however, although like the Tiger's blind flying panel consisting of an air speed indicator, turn and bank indicator and altimeter, had three extra instruments. These were an artificial horizon, a rate of climb indicator and a directional gyroscope. This apparently was the standard blind flying panel found on every RAF aeroplane of the time. The main instrument was the artificial horizon with its cross wires in the form of an aeroplane's wings which adopted whatever attitude the actual aeroplane was in against a fixed image on the dial. If the aeroplane banked to the left the cross wires tilted to the right, if the nose dropped in a dive so the cross wires would rise above the fixed icon. This gave the pilot a good pictorial image of what the aeroplane was actually doing and he could use his controls to keep those cross wires level and on target all the time. The directional gyroscope seemed a bit of a bind rather than a virtue over the normal compass. It 'recessed' I was told, which meant that every few minutes it had to be reset if it were to remain accurate. Its virtue was that it did not undershoot and overshoot with the lag and over-response of the ordinary compass when going through north and south headings.

My first exercise was to fly for five minutes on each cardinal heading, that is north, east, south and west, finishing hopefully where I had started. The trace I created on paper failed to meet the starting point however, missing it by a fraction. The instructor told me that this was because I had edged off to starboard after the first course.

With the weather still clamped down I made my second visit to the Link Trainer the next day. This time I had to fly eight different courses, north, south east, south west, north west, north east (a long course), north west, south west and south east, which on paper completed a figure of eight. I must have held my courses much more accurately this time because I was very little out in completing the figure. Although I felt exhausted as I climbed out of the Link the instructor seemed quite pleased with the result.

As we walked back from the Link Block, George Thame put his hand on my shoulder and said, "You never go to the Red Cow with the lads, Dennis, yet I know you're not TT. Why is that? Do you have scruples or something?" I laughed. George did tend to treat me like his younger brother sometimes. "No George, no scruples." I was thoughtful for a few steps.

"Yes, well I suppose I have really. Do you know, I have never been in a pub in all my life." George's thick eyebrows went up even further than normal. "Why?"

"I don't know. I've never thought about it really, but I don't think much of anyone who can drink so much as to lose their self-control." In retrospect, of course, I was doing no more than echo the sort of sentiments my mother had always preached. She often told the story of how her brother had once overturned the dinner table in a drunken frenzy to illustrate her abhorrence of alcohol. It obviously had made an enormous impression upon her as a young Victorian girl and to hear it myself as a young lad of seven or so it probably had a strong effect upon me too.

"But you don't have to get drunk. I don't get drunk every time I go into a pub. It's a sociable activity, to go and have a beer with your friends."

"OK. George, I'll have a drink with you this evening in the mess." "You're on Dennis lad, you're on - but you're paying!"

I shut the door behind me in my bedroom and went over and sat on the bed. "Really Mum, times change. I promise I won't turn the table over!"

I recalled going to the pictures with Mum and Dad when I was about ten years old. While Mum and I waited outside, Dad popped in to a pub for a quick beer before rejoining us and taking us on to the cinema in Rye Lane. Mum never said anything in my hearing but I knew only too well how much she disapproved. Poor Dad. He only wanted a harmless half pint. He never went on a drunken binge in his life and I never saw him even slightly merry.

CHAPTER 9

The weather cleared at last on Tuesday and we reported to the dispersal in the morning for flying. I had two fifty-minute trips with P.O Tillet. The cloud was thin, puffy cumulus, about four-tenths, that is it covered about four-tenths of the sky with bright blue in between. The wind seemed quite strong and no doubt responsible for having blown away the rain of the last few days.

I taxied the aeroplane out to the take off position and found it quite a strenuous activity. It needed hefty heaves on the rudder bar to swing the nose around in the required fashion. It was a relief to take off and cool down in the slipstream. We climbed up to two thousand feet and Tillet levelled out.

"OK. Berry, you've got it. Keep it straight and level."

We were well below the cloud base, but the ride today was much bumpier than the first day had been. Every so often it felt as if something had physically bumped the aeroplane and it would rise a few feet and then drop again with stomach-lurching suddenness. There was a good clear horizon though and I managed to keep the nose on it, or thereabouts.

"OK. Let's try some climbing and gliding now. I've got it." I let go the stick, "You've got it."

"With straight and level flight, cruising that is, we have around eighteen or nineteen hundred revs. But for climbing we need to open the throttle to two thousand one hundred revs." The throttle moved forward slightly.

"Now raise the nose by pulling the control column back until the speed falls off to sixty-five miles an hour and then adjust the tail trimmer so that the aeroplane maintains this attitude." I tried visually to fix the position of the nose and wings in this climbing attitude with relation to the horizon. Tillet throttled back and dropped the nose on to the horizon once more.

"Now you have a go. You've got it."

I went through the drill of opening the throttle, pulling the nose up and re-trimming. I found the most difficult bit was keeping the airspeed at sixty-five, but once I had set the trim correctly this maintained itself. We were nudging the cloud base at this stage with wispy grey streaks whipping past the wing struts. Tillet told me to level out.

Gliding was simply the reverse of climbing, I found. It was also done at sixty-five miles an hour, with a readjustment of the trim once again and with the throttle closed. But then followed the manoeuvre I was not looking forward to - stalling. I knew that this is where, with insufficient forward speed to give the necessary lift, the aeroplane literally falls out of the sky. It is taught to pilots so that they can recognise the condition as it approaches and to teach them how to recover from it when it happens.

We were flying now at just over two thousand feet. Tillet had control and he went through a careful procedure of circling and peering down over the side of the cockpit to be sure that no other aeroplane was directly below us.

"Now, I close the throttle and slowly pull the nose up. The speed falls off, 75 - 65 - 55 - 50 and look, the controls are getting very floppy," and he was churning the stick around furiously with no apparent effect whatsoever, " - 45 -" and then suddenly with a stomach-lurching whoosh the nose flopped and we were mushing down like a flat pancake, completely out of control. Tillet's voice came through loud and clear, "To recover, push the stick forward and hold it there until the speed builds up and you regain control... If a wing drops in the stall, kick on opposite rudder, but only after you have pushed the stick right forward."

Tillet explained later on the ground that with the stick back the elevators tend to mask the rudder and it becomes less effective in picking up a wing, hence the importance of thrusting the stick right forward before applying opposite rudder.

"Of course, if you don't pick up a wing when it drops in a stall, you'll go into a spin. We'll be doing spinning a bit later and you'll see what I mean."

It was now my turn to stall the aeroplane and after Tillet had once again checked that no one was below us he handed control over. This second stall was not quite so terrifying, probably because I was doing it myself, but even so my stomach was up in my mouth as I thrust the stick forward, then as the speed built, up I pulled it gently back, opened the throttle and raised the nose up to the horizon again.

The cadets were all going along so far at the same pace, but those who went up first to practice a new manoeuvre would come back to tell the others of the horrors in store. I enjoyed telling the waiting cadets how in a stall there is a complete loss of control and the aeroplane suddenly plunges down towards the ground with imminent danger of flicking over into a deadly spin. I was very glad I had gone up first and did not have to listen to that particular line-shoot myself.

On the next trip that morning we started practising medium turns. Tillet went through the theory first on the ground and for such a purpose they had a large model aeroplane at the dispersal. One frequently saw an instructor with his pupil standing outside 'flying' this model aeroplane through various manoeuvres. He explained that so far the movements of the controls I had experienced were all with respect to the aeroplane flying straight and level, "That is, you pull the stick back to make the nose pitch up above the horizon and push the rudder bar to make the nose yaw right or left on the horizon. But if you bank the aeroplane steeply these controls are reversed in that now you have to push the rudder bar to make the nose pitch up or down on the horizon and pull the stick back to make the nose yaw round the horizon. In a medium turn you are half-way between these two states, so as you bank over with the stick to one side you have to pull slightly back as well as putting on a bit of rudder to get the nose going round."

"It sounds more complicated than it really is as you will see, but what it boils down to is fine co-ordination between all the controls. And that's what flying is all about really, co-ordination - relaxing and co-ordinating the controls. After a bit you'll feel when things are

61

wrong and make the necessary adjustments - by reflex. They call it flying by the seat of the pants, and that's what it really is all about."

We took off for me to try and put all this wisdom to good effect. It really was easier than it had sounded, because I found that very small adjustments only were necessary to keep the nose on the horizon in the turn. The turn and bank indicator was vital as well and I found that a slight nudge on the rudder quickly centred the top needle every time it wandered off. As Tillet had said, I also found that I felt comfortable all the time the top needle was centred, but when it edged off to one side or the other in a turn I felt as if I was skidding or slipping out of the cockpit - very uncomfortable. I could see how one might be able to fly on these sensations alone and without the instrument, "Like riding a bike really.... Yes, that's a good analogy," I thought. "Not bad after two and a half hours flying."

We walked back to the mess for lunch, having dumped our parachutes back in the section on the way. The talk was - as ever - about flying. We discussed the morning's experiences, some with embroidery, some with understatement, but all with enthusiasm. We were all here with a driving ambition to fly and to fight. We were young in life and experience and war was, as yet, untasted and still a glamorous adventure for us. The way ahead led only to glory. The Battle of Britain had been fought by the likes of us, with the exception that they were all amazing heroes, but there was still a war to be won and with a bit of luck we should be able to get into it in time. It was a justifiable war too. We had to stop that maniac Hitler from over-running the free world and from committing his further nameless atrocities upon the Jews - and from our own families here in England!

The flying instructors had already assumed the status in our eyes of gods, with their laconic attitudes, their friendliness towards us, but above all for the precision and brilliance of their flying. Each cadet thought of his instructor as the finest pilot in the air force. Without knowing their history it was assumed that they had all flown fighters - Spits undoubtedly - had probably downed numerous enemy and were now doing this tour of instructing by way of recuperation. Flight Lieutenant Spencer was evidence of this after all, what with his DFC, his nervous twitch and the awful burn scars. It was a powerful incentive to do well and to show them how good a pilot you too would be. There was even Flight Lieutenant Knock to inspire us, a white-haired veteran from the 1914/1918 war, with his Royal Flying Corps Wings and his Distinguished Flying Cross.

The afternoon ground school was a good opportunity to imbibe some theory, although it was understood that the exams at the end of the course did not carry much weight compared to the flying. The Link Trainer was seen as being very relevant too, although as time went on it began to be viewed as a chore, necessary but tedious, like PT.

I was on Link that afternoon and I had to fly a number of compass courses. I was not very good, however, wandering off too much and overturning, that is turning too far past the heading I was going for. I guess I felt tired and my concentration was obviously poor. We spent the next afternoon at flight dispersal and I got in another two trips. On both Tillet took me up to practice climbing, gliding and medium turns and apart from the actual take-offs and landings I did most of the flying. It was very bumpy below the cloud base though and Tillet took over and climbed up through a gap in the puffy cumulus. The clouds were about four to five hundred feet thick from their grey level base, up to the top of their white rolling heads. It was a breath-catching moment as we emerged above the brilliant white clouds and into a dome of pure ultramarine. I looked around, the vast tablecloth of cloud from horizon to horizon was like a drenched sea of foam. The sky above was intensely blue shading down to a golden paleness where it met the clouds. The slipstream felt icy at this altitude, but it was wonderful for flying, smooth and with a perfect horizon.

CHAPTER 10

There was no flying the next morning. The wind was too strong, kicking the windsocks up past the horizontal and rattling the hangar doors fretfully. This meant no flying at all that day because Wednesday afternoons were reserved for flying personnel to do organised games. There were two squash courts on the station as well as a couple of tennis courts, but these did not go very far among the instructors and cadets who wanted to use them. Some played a scratch game of football, others ran round the airfield perimeter, a select few went off for a round of golf and the rest did PT. I did PT. I would have liked to have played golf, but in the absence of clubs this would have been difficult. So, after I had finished dancing up and down on the hangar apron and generally working up a sweat, I had a shower and then got down on my bed to luxuriate in a snooze before 1730 hours and tea - as the evening meal was called.

I had lots to write home and tell Joan about and I intended to do just that, although it could be difficult sometimes to escape from the other lads and the general nattering that went on in the mess in the evening.

I had met Joan in Sittingbourne after the family had been evacuated from London. I had walked into the Paper Mill one day and asked if they had a job. They took me up to see Mr Kemsley, the General Manager, who seemed to take a liking to me, because he offered me a job on the spot to work in the Accounts Department. Old Mr Denny however, the Manager of Accounts, really had no idea what to do with this lad who had no experience of accounting, invoicing, despatch, shipping, insurance, or anything else that went on in his domain. So he put me in charge of Stationery.

Within three months I had organised a mini-empire for myself. Instructions were issued to all departments establishing the new rules for ordering stationery along with the necessary indents - in triplicate - the stationery store was re-arranged to enable a desk to be located in it, plus a telephone, and numerous stationery manufacturers and suppliers were informed that henceforth they would be tendering competitively if they wanted to supply Edward Lloyd Limited. Old Mr Denny never commented on the revolution that hit his pencil and paper clip department, but Mr Kemsley was tickled pink about it.

"It's the sought of ginger we need around here sometimes," he confided once, perhaps a touch thoughtlessly, to his elderly secretary.

Joan Wyver was a typist working with two or three other girls in the typing pool. She and her particular friend Mavis soon noticed this new boy in Accounts - after all, he was different from the average type one generally found in Sittingbourne. Mavis was already going out with John, a lad in Accounts, and so between them they arranged to fix me up to make a foursome with Joan. It was all great fun really; Joan was a quiet although very intelligent girl and we got on together extremely well.

We used to meet up at Edward Lloyd's Social Club, play table tennis and even dabble in the Amateur Dramatic Society. Joan and I soon decided that we were more interested in each other than in doing things with the other two, so we gradually split up as a foursome. I was very happy. It was my first experience with an adult girl friend and one whom I could take home and introduce as such.

We saw each other most nights, walking out into the country and talking seriously about politics, the war and the future. We discovered that we were both passionate socialists and made great plans for a beautiful Britain after the war. I admired Joan's mind, she was well educated with Higher School Certificate and should have gone on to university but for a personal quirk of wanting to start work straight away. Frequently an air raid would start as we walked and we would watch the searchlights pencilling across the night sky and the occasional star-like dots of exploding ack-ack shells. Once a hot piece of shrapnel as big as a half crown pattered across our feet, but it did not register as any sort of hazard. We were obviously in love! Indeed, the seat within the church porch at Tunstel became our most important rendezvous.

Joan was quite obsessive about making something of her life and of getting out of Sittingbourne and when I asked her if she would like to get married she took it as a proposal and said yes. We were sitting in the Odeon cinema when it happened; it was during the interval. I couldn't think of anything to say immediately. I squeezed her hand tightly. It was OK. I'd like to get married. I did love her. And that was how it happened.

We said nothing to anyone about it at the time, but agreed to wait until I had got my wings before actually getting hitched. I first mentioned it to Mum when I wrote home from Initial Training Wing in Paignton. Getting my wings seemed a long way ahead at that stage, but it seemed to be a good point to aim for. Neither of us talked very much about what might happen after that.

The morning of the 10th was bright, clear and fresh and although the wind was still quite strong it had now lessened. The black and white flag was flying which meant dual only, but by the afternoon when I was on flying this had ameliorated slightly and the white flag was up - not that I anticipated going solo. "A lovely afternoon for circuits and bumps," was how the prop-swinger greeted us. He was right too. Tillet called me out.

"Let's go and do some take-offs and landings, OK?" I followed him out to the plane. Quite a few of the others had already started on landings and I certainly did not want to fall behind.

The take-off was reasonably familiar by now and Tillet reminded me to get the tail up into the flying position as soon as possible and to keep the nose straight on a point on the boundary of the airfield. "OK Berry, take off and climb up to a thousand feet." We were sitting crosswind on the boundary already and so I went straight into the pre-flight cockpit check using the prescribed pneumonic T T M F S S.

"Throttle nut - tightened, Trim - set for take-off (two-thirds forward), Mixture - rich, Fuel - on, Switches - on, Slots - unlocked." Then with elaborate caution (and thumping heart) I peered downwind to make sure no other plane was landing nearby, very aware that Tillet was watching me closely in his mirror. A quick glance upwind to make sure the take-off path was clear and I edged the throttle open applying full right rudder to swing the nose into wind.

This was it. Holding the stick right back in my stomach, I pushed the throttle fully open. The plane started rolling forward and I felt the acceleration pressing me back in the seat. Coarse movements on the rudder to keep the nose straight and then the fight to stop the swing to the right as the speed increases. Stick right forward to get the tail up - hold it there - keep straight with the rudder - bump - bump - bump - the noise at its maximum - stick back slightly and - ah - peace as the wheels unstick - hold it there just above the ground - speed up to 65 and then ease the nose up and set the trimmer for climbing.

"Don't forget to throttle back," Tillet reminded as we went through 500 feet. He was quite pleased with his pupil's first effort. "You over-controlled a bit ... too heavy on the stick. You must learn to relax. Hold the stick lightly. OK, I've got it. I'll now take you round the circuit and show you a glide approach and landing."

On the downwind leg past the airfield, one had to make a decision about turning across wind, closing the throttle, gliding down to 500 feet and then turning in to land. All this was to be done at the right heights and distances otherwise one would undershoot or overshoot the field. It was logical to identify landmarks to mark the turning points and I guess I did my best to do this, but the theory was much easier than the practice. It was the landing itself however, which was the real pig to master. Tillet demonstrated it perfectly.

"Hold the aeroplane in the glide, right down to about twenty feet. Now check the descent and level out. Hold the plane at this height, and as the speed falls off move the stick back, gently - gently - the plane sinks lower and lower and just above the ground - now - pull the stick right back and it stalls down on to all three points at once."

It was a perfect landing, the wheels and tailskid gently kissing the grass. It all seemed so easy and yet it was incredibly difficult to do, that is to do as sweetly as that. Tillet turned across wind at the end of the landing run, paused to check no one was landing nearby and then taxied back to the perimeter.

"OK Berry, now you take off, do the circuit and try a landing."

My first attempt was awful. I got the plane round and more or less down in the landing position, about halfway across the field, but tried to land it about twenty feet up in the air. If Tillet had not taken over at the last moment we would have bent the undercarriage at least, if not written the entire plane off. The next attempt was better, in that we were lower, but finished up just rolling the wheels along the ground without holding off and stalling it down. The third attempt was diabolical. I got the circuit wrong and we overshot. Tillet took over even as I was trying to level out almost on the opposite boundary.

"Now, come on Berry, you could see you'd never get in at that height." He whipped the plane round the circuit, put it on the correct crosswind leg and handed over to me to complete the landing. This one was better, but it was still a 'wheelie'.

We went up again later and did two more circuits and bumps, but I was still having trouble judging my height and identifying the moment the aeroplane stalled. On the second one of the landings I held off, misjudged the stall and pulled the stick back too early, pulling the nose right up. We were hanging on the prop at an angle of fortyfive degrees and at a height of about twentyfive feet, the classic novice landing. If Tillet had not rammed the throttle open and pushed the nose down we would have been so much bent spars and canvas in the middle of the field.

The buzz in the mess was now all about landings. A few of the lads were happy and feeling they were getting the hang of it, but many, like me, were far more gloomy. Bob Eaves, Tillet's other pupil, sounded as if he was getting on famously. He certainly thought that Tillet was a wonderful Instructor.

"He's brilliant. Did you see the way he put it down when the tea van arrived? He sideslipped over the dispersal, straightened out and put it down next to the van. That's flying." While loyal in front of the others, I felt a niggling reservation about him. "It's probably because I'm not coping very well yet," I thought.

I was on flying again the next morning and had two more trips with Tillet, getting in four circuits and landings on the first trip. On the second flight Tillet asked me to climb up to 5,000 feet, the highest I had ever been. There was some thin cloud at 3,000 but with plenty of gaps through which to fly. Once above the cloud, which was only a few hundred feet thick, everything was brilliant sunshine and looking down through the cloud gaps the normally green fields began to take on a blue hazy quality. At 5,000 feet, as we levelled out, I felt a new sensation of remoteness; the earth was barely visible in the haze and it was impossible to pick out any detail on the ground. It felt quite lonely under this vast blue dome. The aeroplane seemed to be poised motionless with no sensation of speed whatsoever, only the sun glinting in the arc of the propeller - and it was very cold indeed.

"OK, I've got it." Tillet's cheerful voice broke the spell. "This is enough height for us to do some spinning, OK? Lock the slots first will you." He waited for my confirmation that I had done this.

"First we have to make quite sure that there is no one underneath us," and he circled steeply peering down over the side of the cockpit.

"Now, to spin we have to close the throttle, pull the nose up and at the point of the stall pull the stick right back and push on full rudder in the direction in which you want to spin. This stalls that wing and over you go. To recover, you push the stick right forward and then apply opposite rudder. As the plane stops spinning, you take off the rudder and gently pull the nose back up on to the horizon and open the throttle. OK?" I managed a "yes" response, although I felt far from OK! I squirmed down as low as I could in the cockpit and braced myself much as one would on a wild fairground ride.

Tillet cut the throttle, the nose started to rise and that unfamiliar quietness took over the aeroplane as it approached the stall. Suddenly the left wing dropped, the horizon appeared over my left shoulder angling and turning and then all I could see were the fields rotating rapidly round and round in front of the nose. It was an extremely violent motion and I was pressed sideways in my harness, the world spinning madly in front of me. Just as suddenly, the spinning stopped and momentarily we were diving vertically downwards – then, feeling as if I was being pressed through my seat by gravity, I saw the nose rise up to the horizon.

"Let's climb back up to 5,000 feet again and then you can have a go."

I wished I had joined the navy.

I went through the circling routine, checking that all was clear below and then settled myself down in the cockpit for the coming ordeal. The spin when it happened again astonished me by its suddenness. One moment we were hanging on the prop apparently motionless and the next we were in the violent gyrating madhouse spinning earthwards. It was amazing how the frail aeroplane withstood such violence. We recovered after only one complete turn in the spin and I dragged the nose back up to normality. My shortness of reach on the pedals did not make the spin recovery any easier. I found that I had to extend my foot almost to tiptoe to get full opposite rudder on. I suppose I really was only just tall enough to fly in the RAF. The manoeuvre illustrated for me, if nothing else had done so far, the need to have my Sutton Harness belted up as tightly as possible before leaving the ground.

On our return to the airfield Tillet demonstrated a power approach and landing. This involved coming in with the engine on rather than gliding in. The approach was flatter and started further out from the boundary and instead of stalling the aeroplane on to the ground, one flew it on, which meant landing on the two wheels only. It was a more controlled landing and therefore easier because of this and was the reason one had to use a glide approach and landing for the purposes of going solo.

I entered the spinning exercise in my logbook in red ink as prescribed. The RAF liked its pilots to practice spinning recovery regularly for obvious safety reasons. I added up my flying time and found that it was now a total of six and a half hours dual. "Four more hours to go," I thought with just the faintest stirrings of panic.

The next morning, Sunday the 12th, was Church Parade. At 0900 hours the entire station, apart from the guard and other denominations, had to form up on the hangar apron. The CO, Wing Commander Beaumont, took the salute and then the Padre took the service. For the first time in my career I realised why it was a good idea not to be C of E.

"It's really the only bit of bull here at Desford, you shouldn't complain," George said, very surprised at my strength of feeling. "Look, the Old Man's loving it. The only time he gets at being CO."

After the Church Parade was dismissed I had to report to the Link Block for a couple of sessions. This time I found I was required to maintain a given airspeed and height while flying a number of short courses and then on to a variety of climbing and losing altitude exercises. It was obviously very good practice in instrument flying, but it did get very tedious sitting under that hood and concentrating on those instruments for an hour.

I flew a couple of trips that afternoon and again the following morning, all on circuits and bumps - another two hours and fifty minutes to add to my total. Then on the afternoon of the 14th I had one more trip with PO Tillet, doing four more circuits without any great improvement in the landings, which brought me up to the dreaded ten hours dual - and no solo! As we walked back to the dispersal from the aeroplane Tillet told me not to worry.

"I think you are nearly there. It's the last holding off, judging your height and getting the feel of the plane on the point of the stall. It'll come, don't worry," and he bustled off with his usual nervous haste.

"In other words, he could have said 'you haven't got the faintest idea'!" I thought miserably as I walked in, despondent, worried and frustrated.

"Why can't I do it? If only he weren't in the front there." The first one on the course to solo had gone off a couple of days ago, after only seven and a half hours. He had his check with the flight commander and we saw Wynne-Powell take the stick out of the front cockpit and send him off. We all crowded outside to watch him taxi round the perimeter and then stand crosswind for ages. We saw him turn into wind, kick his tail up as he belted across the field and then pull up into his climb. Every man watching was with him, we all felt his loneliness in that small aeroplane as it jinked upwards in the wind. We watched him among the dozen other planes as he flew round the circuit - in such company yet especially alone - and then we moved out on to the grass to look back downwind at him gliding in towards the field. His approach looked alright, wings wobbling a bit as the gusting wind caught them, but no problems. In fact he made a good landing and we all cheered loudly with relief.

Flight Sergeant Brett sending a pupil on his first solo
Photograph courtesy of the Imperial War Museum, London

I had one more trip with Tillet the next afternoon and as we walked in Tillet said, "I've asked Sergeant Harry to take you up, Berry. It might just do the trick for you." Sergeant Harry was younger than Tillet and although I had not spoken with him before, he was extremely friendly and put his hand on my shoulder as we walked out to his plane. It all seemed very ominous however and I began to feel sick in my stomach. Four more circuits without much improvement and morale sank even lower.

I had two further trips with Sergeant Harry the next morning, going up to do some more spinning on the first one before returning to the circuits and landings on the second. The wind was very strong though and I was extremely tense as I struggled to counter the buffeting. The prop-swingers came out to greet us as we taxied in, one on each wing, to stop the plane from arrowing into the wind.

I counted the hours in my logbook - twelve hours and twenty minutes. "Oh God, I'm not going to do it." I closed my eyes. "Mum will be glad I suppose." I thought of Joan, of our great plans when I got my wings. "I've got to bloody do it." I knew now how Ron must have felt when he washed out.

Thursday 16th October dawned very clear and bright, too bright it seemed, for by 0900 the wind was gusting across the field and threatening to rip the Tigers off their moorings and to fray the windsocks from their masts. It was black flag weather for flying kites but good for flying the Link. I had two lessons and as if to compensate for my failure in the Tiger I flew the kiwi bird very well.

The white flag was up the next morning, the wind having dropped overnight and we all reported out to our flights. An officer instructor came in to the dispersal and called out for LAC Berry. He smiled at me as I stood up and told me he was taking me over. I liked the look of him. He was quite old - at least twenty-five that is - with short cropped hair greying at the sides and warm smiling eyes beneath bushy grey eyebrows. Pilot Officer Vaughan took me out straightaway for a flight which lasted just under the hour. We got in six landings, mainly by virtue of the way Vaughan took over from me as soon as I had taken off, whipped us around a very hairy circuit at a few hundred feet and handed back over to me again on the cross-wind leg. Vaughan did not say much, but he was very patient and encouraging. Whether it was this, or the condensed landing practice, but I felt more confident as we came in. I had another quick trip with Vaughan later in the morning and managed to get in another three landings. But they were apparently still not good enough to justify a solo and I was now desperately worried. I had done thirteen hours and forty-five minutes dual and this was far more than was normally allowed.

Link practice that afternoon had me flying without the ASI and with the Gyro Compass and the Artificial Horizon hooded. The instructor told me I did very well. "I can fly the Tiger quite well too, it's only the bloody landings I can't do!"

There followed two fraught and utterly miserable days. The wind was up again to gale force and there was no flying on either day. "It is just my luck - Sod's law. I believe I nearly had it last Friday and now I'm going to have to start all over again - If I get the chance that is." "No you won't. The rest will do you good, you'll see." I was not comforted. Already six had been washed out from the course out of the fifty who had started and there were others sweating like me. By Monday morning the gales had subsided and the white flag was flying. Vaughan had me out for the first trip and we just did the one circuit and landing. It was not too bad.

"You're down for a Flight Commander's Test this morning, Berry. Nothing to worry about. Just do another circuit like that last one. And - good luck." He smiled and nodded reassuringly. The prospect of a Flight Commander's Test at any time was grim enough, but to have one now with fourteen hours dual in my logbook could only mean one thing – washout!

I waited miserably for the call. There was no escape. This was it. "I can simply do my best." Fl Lt Wynne-Powell seemed preoccupied when he finally did appear and asked me to go out to his plane. He was kindly enough however, when he joined me.

"We are going up to see how well you are getting on. It's a lovely day for flying and I want you to settle down and show me what you can do. As soon as you are ready, start up and then take off and climb up to two thousand feet." Thereafter he did not say another word until we were at altitude. I was going through the procedures as carefully as I knew how, watching my air speed like a hawk, correcting every deviation of the Turn and Bank as delicately as possible and holding the stick as if it were made of glass.

Wynne-Powell then had me doing some medium turns in both directions, before asking me to climb up to three thousand feet to demonstrate stalls and recovery. I felt that I performed these

74

reasonably well and was beginning to enjoy myself when Wynne-Powell told me to return to the aerodrome and land.

My approach was OK, clearing the boundary by forty or fifty feet, gliding across the field to about a third of the way in, holding off nicely - and then not a bad landing, almost a three pointer. I swung across wind as we came to rest and then taxied back towards the nearest boundary anticipating another circuit and landing. Wynne-Powell stopped me however,

"No, taxi back to the dispersal." My heart plunged into my boots and I momentarily closed his eyes. "It's not bloody fair." I thought as I taxied slowly back. I swung the aeroplane into wind and was about to put my hand out to switch off, when Wynne-Powell's Sutton Harness straps came sailing over his head and I saw him climbing out on to the wing. Then he turned and leaned back to rummage in his cockpit for a few seconds. When he came up again he was holding the joystick!

"Off you go, one circuit and landing, that's all," and he waved the stick happily at me, grinning broadly as he climbed down off the wing.

I taxied out my heart bursting. I couldn't believe it. I was alone in the aeroplane at last. "Now, every thing has got to be done right," and I peered sharply out either side as I swung the nose. I stopped across wind on the boundary and did my cockpit check. Then a careful look down wind, nothing coming in - and with my heart racing I gunned the plane into wind.

"You've got it Berry," and I thrust the throttle fully open. "Here we go ..."

The plane felt so much lighter. It bounced into the air very quickly and I pulled it up into the climb. It was not until I was on the down wind leg that I was able to relax and really savour the moment. It was utterly unbelievable. I was actually up here alone flying this aeroplane on my first solo. I had dreamed about it since I was about eight years old, but I never thought it would really happen.

"There's no PO Vaughan up in front there now to get you out of trouble," and I felt a fleeting zizz of panic. It was quickly gone, submerged in all the other emotions though as I turned across wind past the airfield and cut the throttle. Re-trim - it was done automatically.

"Now, push the nose down, keep the airspeed up, 65 - good. Turn into wind. Hold it ... steady, steady. This should be OK."

The ground came up quickly as I leaned out to the left, one hand on the throttle, the other twitching the stick to counter every deviation of the wings.

"Now," as I checked the glide ... "hold off, hold off, hold off," and then ramming the stick back into my stomach ... the plane sank the last foot and I was down - a near perfect landing.

"I've done it," I screamed, "I've bloody done it."

'First Solo', painted by Dennis Berry, 2002

CHAPTER II

One thing a civilian would never have understood would have been the extent to which the average RAF serviceman was insulated from the war. In contrast, those on the home front were ever depressingly reminded of the conflict by the raids and the rationing - food rationing and that of other essentials like clothing and petrol - plus the total absence, or scarcity, of items previously taken for granted like bananas, lemons, oranges, chocolate, whiskey, and so on. Then there were the queues, queues for everything, from bread to beer and soap to spam, and of course there was the blackout! But perhaps the worst and most constant reminder of the war for those left behind was the absence of their loved ones who had gone off to fight it.

The average RAF serviceman stationed in the UK, for his part, ate regularly and pretty well, in spite of his eternal grumbles. Compared with the civilian, he certainly had more than a fair share of the rationed goods and many servicemen were further spoiled with food parcels from home, food that was eked out from a meagre civilian ration. For those stationed in the Midlands, or further north, they were away from the sleep-disturbing wail of the air raid siren and they rarely saw a newspaper. Such were the hardships suffered by me and many just like me. OK, so we were lucky. I know there were many other poor sods who were not so fortunate.

In my personal battle with the Tiger Moth, I was scarcely aware of the fight continuing in Europe. It is true that the war had moved further away from the shores of this island and was now deep in Russia where the German push to capture Moscow had already lasted for weeks rather than days. Stalin, having declared a state of siege, had issued his order of the day - "Moscow will be defended to the last."

Hitler had four Panzer armies, each with 5,000 tanks, massed along the three hundred mile front. If the war was referred to at all in the Mess at this time, it was when George Thame reminded me that Napoleon began his disastrous retreat from Moscow in 1812 - also in

October! Was it significant that the present battlefield was reported as being covered with a thick carpet of snow?

The other item of news which did filter through to Desford was that the Japanese Prime Minister had resigned and had been succeeded by a General Tojo, reputed to be very anti-America and pro-Germany.

If I was insulated somewhat from the war, I was also insulated from the day-to-day doings at home. No one wrote to tell me of bad news, nor even of unpleasant news. It was always of how well everyone was and of how well everyone was doing. I never received any specific news of Ernest, or about the garage and I was always somehow too diffident to ask, although I did wonder sometimes. In one mood I could admire my brother-in-law for his entrepreneurial skills and his single mindedness, but at other times I knew he was a rogue.

There was that question about the house in Melbourne Grove and whether he was motivated altruistically in saving Dad's bacon, or was he out simply to make himself a few quid? It was never clear, although he did make money in the process, however motivated. It had been in the mid-thirties when trade was at an all-time low. Dad's partner, George Bush, said he could no longer survive on what they were making and withdrew from the partnership, taking with him his personal tools and equipment and leaving Dad the impossible task of running both sides of the business. He too should have got out while there was yet something to save, but he hung on and did his damnedest to make it work. But trade and money got less and less.

Both Rene and Vie were married and there were only we two boys left at home. Ern and Rene came up from Sittingbourne that weekend and the visit finished up with something like a council of war.

"You've got to cut your overheads somehow, Dad."

"Good advice son, but how? We already live on the breadline."
Ernest looked around at the remains of the dinner we had just eaten - roast beef, Yorkshires, three veg and apple pie with custard.

"I'm talking about the Works and about this place. The big expenses. You don't have to live in this enormous house now with

78

just the four of you." Mother snorted, goaded into saying something at last. "We can't move from this beautiful old house. We brought the kids up in it, you were married from here. Where could we go to?" She turned to her daughter for support, but Rene said nothing.

"What about the Works then? If you sold out now you could salvage a hell of a lot, enough to start up again somewhere else - on a smaller scale." Dad looked at him bleakly.

"It might be good advice Ern, but it's my life's work you are talking about."

"I know that man, but you have got to face facts. If you hang on too long you'll go bust and you'll lose everything. What will you do then with nothing salvaged?" Dad shrugged as he played with the crumbs on the tablecloth in front of him.

"Talk to an estate agent, have the place valued. That won't cost you anything." "Selling the business means I sell the income and there wouldn't be anything coming in at all."

"Not for a bit, that's true. But you'd have the capital to tide you over until you got another place - a shop perhaps."

Ernest returned to the subject a couple of weekends later. He said he had been giving the situation a lot of thought. "You will have to sell the business sooner or later and buy something smaller, but immediately, I think you should sell this house." He paused to let the idea sink in. "And if it's going to help, I'll buy it from you. I'll give you seven hundred." His eyes gleamed - just as they did when he was selling a motorcar.

It was probably a reasonable price at the time and Dad accepted it, "Making the best of a very bad job," he said. The fact that Ernest made a few hundred pounds on the eventual resale was not seen as relevant. After all they were keeping the money in the family, weren't they?

Immediately after my first solo, PO Vaughan took me up for a couple of quick circuits and then sent me off by himself to practise my landings. I had barely touched down and returned to the dispersal in time for a drink from the tea van when Vaughan was chasing me out once again for another dual flight. He took me up to barely three thousand feet, demonstrating climbing turns on the way, got me to do two spins and then showed me how to side-slip on the way down.

"This is the only time you legitimately cross your controls, that is to side-slip to the left, apply full right rudder, stick hard to the left and back to pull the nose up." The aeroplane was in a crazy attitude, the left wing down, the nose way up and we were crabbing sideways, the slipstream buffeting straight into the side of the cockpit. It was all done at the gliding speed of sixty-five. It was a simple manoeuvre, but looked very sophisticated in terms of aeroplane control, particularly when an instructor did it coming in over the dispersal to land a few feet away from the tea van. The side-slip would be held until only a few feet from the ground when the controls would be centred and the plane would recover straight into a three-point landing.

I felt immensely happy with the morning. I had been flying for nearly three hours - fifty minutes of it solo! I checked myself nodding off in the Link that afternoon, I felt so bushed.

The intensive pace in flying was kept up during the next few weeks with we cadets usually getting in four flights a session, that is over three hours a day, much of which was solo. The weather held out and PO Vaughan seemed to be taking me through the syllabus at a fast canter - steep turns, instrument flying, low flying, forced landings, precautionary landings, taking off and landing out of wind, map reading, inverted flying and aerobatics. After each demonstration he would send me up to practice the new manoeuvre solo until I could reproduce it to his satisfaction, that is with the exception of instrument flying, which was done blind under the hood, and low flying - forbidden unless with an instructor and over the prescribed area - or that was the theory anyway!

Aerobatics, or dog fighting were a legitimate way of venting high spirits and all the cadets indulged regularly. The loop to be performed accurately meant that one had to fly through one's own slipstream and when you felt the bump you knew you had done it properly. If the loop was sufficiently tight, the centrifugal force kept you comfortably in your seat and you simply peered over the top of your head waiting for the horizon to come up. If it was too loose however, by the time you got it inverted you would be hanging in your straps ready to flop out of the sky, all very uncomfortable. One could develop quite a lot of 'G' in the loop, too, by pulling it very tight, so much so that you could black yourself out in the process, as I discovered.

The slow roll however, was the real test of a pilot's skill in the Tiger Moth. This involved rotating the aircraft through a hundred and eighty degrees on its fore and aft axis and had to be done in a perfectly straight line. One could too easily finish up thirty or forty degrees off course in a badly executed manoeuvre. To fly the aircraft round a slow roll involved the use of the ailerons, the rudder and the elevators, all finely co-ordinated to keep the nose just above the horizon and pinned on a point straight ahead. To be done nicely it required a fair amount of strength and very precise flying by the seat of the pants. It also required longer arms than I really had, especially for a roll to the right, when I would be pushing the stick over away from me to the right hand corner of the cockpit as I hung inverted from my harness. My slow rolls though in fact, were quite good.

I found that it was always possible to establish whether a particular aeroplane had been slow-rolled recently, or not, by the amount of dust and grit that went up past your face as you flew inverted.

I did my first cross-country flight at this time to Mier, dual on the first occasion, after which Vaughan sent me off to do it solo. It was only forty-five minutes' flight time, but it still had to be done as if the destination was up in Scotland. I had to lay out my tracks on the map, with the initial ten degree angles laid off either side for drift correction to the course, and work out the courses to fly allowing for magnetic variation, compass deviations and wind. Finally, I had to estimate my time of arrival. The solo flight went perfectly and I arrived at Mier airfield bang on the nose, getting quite a kick out of landing at another aerodrome and reporting to the Duty Pilot.

We had an unexpected 48 hour pass shortly after this on 8/9th November and I made it home late on the Saturday evening. The family made a tremendous fuss of me. Vie came over from Maidstone on the Sunday, with young Michael, bringing a welcome gift of tobacco and the less-welcome news that Ron was extremely cheesed off having just been posted to Glasgow for yet another course. Joan and I went for a long walk on the Sunday morning and came back with the announcement that we wanted to get married on the first leave after I had got my wings.

"The course should finish late December, or early January, depending upon the weather. I then get posted to a Service Flying Training School which should last about twelve weeks and if I pass it I then get my wings. So that makes it sometime in early, or mid April, say a mid-April wedding." Everyone thought this would be good timing and a lot of the weekend was then spent discussing arrangements.

"We can go and talk to the Vicar, Joan, about the banns," Mother said, "and I must also talk to your Mother about the guest list and so on." This prompted the plea from both Joan and me for - "A quiet wedding please!"

"It can't be anything but in wartime, I'm afraid."

As I was about to leave the house on the Monday evening, I discovered I was out of cigarettes. Ernest, who had just come in, immediately produced a packet of twenty Players and gave them to me. As I turned away muttering my thanks, Ernest said, "1/6d please." I had to borrow the money from Dad to pay him. I thought about it in the train afterwards and I could not decide whether my feelings of resentment were justified or not.

The weather was atrocious over the next few days and there was no flying. Our gloom was further heightened by the news which seeped through the normal service insulation about the sinking of the Ark Royal. Although this achievement had been claimed by the Axis so many times in the past, this time it really was true, a fact made even less palatable by the knowledge that it was a despised Italian torpedo which did it.

I flew again on the 15th when Vaughan took me up to go through the procedure for restarting the engine in flight. This seemed

82

to me to be an over-dramatic operation for such an unlikely event as an engine stoppage, especially when it took such an effort to stop the propeller from going round in the first place. Having switched off the petrol and the engine, Vaughan then literally had to hang the aeroplane on the prop to stop it rotating in the slipstream. Having eventually stalled the fan, it all felt positively weird with the aeroplane gliding so silently, the slipstream whistling through the struts. We were at 6,000 feet and the ground was invisible in the haze. Vaughan put it into a steep dive and held it as the speed built up rapidly - 80, 90, 100, 110, 115, 120 - the petrol and the switches were now on - and as the slip-stream began to screech through the rigging I saw the prop suddenly twitch and then whirl into life as the engine fired and it was all back to business as usual. We were directly above the aerodrome so that had the engine not restarted Vaughan could have made a dead stick landing safely enough. Even so, it was all a bit scary, like asking for trouble?

On our return to the dispersal I heard the gen about an early posting. "Wynne-Powell says we have to get our sixty hours in before Wednesday and they're chasing everyone up into the air." This was reinforced that evening back in the Mess, when there was a lot of talk about an SFTS posting coming through. There was something in the wind; ten pupils had already been told they were going to Canada to do their Service Flying Training. The uncertainty about it was unsettling. One knew the course had to end and that this would be followed by a posting somewhere, but when the rumours started unexpectedly like this, halfway through the course, it was very disturbing.

I did a triangular cross-country the following day, with another instructor, Sergeant Harry, in the front seat. I flew to Cottesmore via Ratcliffe and return. Flying was washed out literally, for the next couple of days, with low cloud and rain. It was just as well that we had a visiting ENSA Concert Party on the second evening to keep the spirits up. The quality of the ENSA concerts, while not up to West End production standards, was always professional and the members did their job by researching a few notable personalities on the station and then including the in-jokes, which always went down well.

We flew on the 21st again, although the cloud base was still very low. I did another cross-country, but this time on instruments, that is flying blind under the hood. Obviously I could not make any corrections to my courses if I had allowed for an incorrect wind to start with, and I had to fly on compass and then alter courses on my stopwatch. I finished up remarkably close to my intended destination, more by luck than judgement, and got a nod and a smile of approval from Vaughan. It certainly developed one's confidence in the instruments.

Blind Flying
Photograph courtesy of the Imperial War Museum, London

We were down for night flying that evening and everyone reported for briefing at 1700. We were given the weather report which spoke of a freshening wind as the night advanced and that there was no moon so it would be very dark. Then the officer in charge of night flying told us how we would be restricted to the circuit, but that in the event of straying off the circuit and getting lost the Chance Light, a very powerful beacon, would be switched on. He also told us that in the event of an air raid the flare path would be extinguished and we should then circle a beacon at a given altitude a few miles due south of the airfield. This raised a few eyebrows and a question about navigation lights. We were told these should be switched off in such an event, otherwise we would be flying with nav lights on.

The aerodrome had an entirely new character that night with the noise of aero engines being run up on the hangar apron, the reflection from the flare path out in the middle of the field and the sound of voices and activity where normally everything was silent and dark. We reported in full flying gear to the pilots' room at the foot of the Control Tower at 2000 hrs. The room was lit by a single low-powered red bulb and was so gloomy that it took some minutes to adjust to the apparent darkness. It was certainly too dark to read and one could only sit and talk or, in the small hours of the night, snooze.

I was down to fly with a Flying Officer Brett, whom I had not met before. I found him to be a very tall, schoolmasterish, elderly man with a strong jutting jaw - elderly, that is about thirty, I thought. Brett told me that we would be doing power approach landings as this enabled a better sight of the flare path and greater control over landing without undershoot or overshoot. It was a very dark moonless night and Brett told me that the flare path was just about all we would see.

The aeroplanes had navigation lights as well as a signalling light on the underside of the fuselage and the drill was to taxi out to a blue light by the flare-path and there to ask for permission to take off by flashing the letter of the day. The Control Pilot stationed at the flare-path would then give you a green or red Aldis depending upon whether you could take off, or not.

I found it very disturbing to start with, taxiing ahead into pitch darkness towards a single blue light, with the stabbing orange-blue exhaust flames reflecting up from the grass beneath the right hand engine cowling. I found it necessary to turn the rheostat for the instrument lights right down to prevent dazzle as we taxied out. We paused by the blue holding light and I asked permission to take off. We received a green and Brett gunned the plane on to the flare path. It receded away ahead of us in perfect flat perspective and as we took off and climbed up from it so the perspective of lights steepened and shortened dramatically until we left it behind. There was no horizon visible and flying was strictly on instruments only. We seemed to be hanging motionless in total blackness and it was not until we had turned downwind that the glimmer from the shielded lights of the flare path became visible once more. In this position, on the down wind leg, I had to flash the letter of the day to get permission to land and this came up promptly as another green Aldis.

The landing itself was fascinating; never having seen a film, or simulation, of a flare path landing, the experience was almost magical. It worked so beautifully, the distant array of lights gradually foreshortening, flattening and finally levelling as we touched down made me chuckle with delight. I did three circuits and landings myself, all commendably safe and looked forward to another flight later that night. The wind gusted up as predicted however, and flying was abandoned before we got to it.

Ground School examinations were due to start on the coming Monday which meant that the day off on Sunday had to be spent swotting. We did fly on the Monday morning though and before reporting to the GI Block at 1400. The exams lasted over the next three days - Navigation (plotting), Navigation (theory), Airmanship, Armaments, Signals and Aircraft Recognition. I felt reasonably happy with my efforts but still very relieved when the results were published a couple of days later. I came tenth overall out of fortyfive and with the individual subject results of 91/100 Navigation (plotting), 75/100 Navigation (theory), 100/120 Airmanship, 90/100 Armaments, 95/100 Signals and 95/100 Aircraft Recognition.

We resumed flying on the following Monday and I gave vent to my feelings after the previous week's tensions with forty minutes of aerobatics going through the full syllabus from stall turns and slow rolls to rolls off the top. I wrote home about this time, saying how much I was enjoying flying.

"When I first started I used to get a bit nervous before each flight, but now it's getting almost commonplace - like driving a car. I would seriously like to carry on flying commercially after the war."

If instrument flying at this stage was the biggest bind then low flying was the favourite. It was supposed to be done at a height of no less than 250 feet, but hedgehopping and tree clipping was much more to the liking of the instructors and pupils both. Most of the pupils indulged in a bit of solo low flying at some time or other, but they were certainly running grave risks of being washed out in the process. I contravened badly one day when I was sent up to do some aerobatics. I found it very misty up to 4,000 feet and then it was just like flying above cloud, so I came down again to about 500 feet and flew across to the low flying area which included the hamlet of Market Bosworth. Here I started doing stall turns at 500 feet and then diving down to near roof height before pulling up. I could see a woman in a garden hanging washing up on a line, her white face upturned watching me. She could have taken my number very easily. It was extremely exhilarating, but also extremely stupid and as I flew back to Desford I chided myself, half expecting to be sent for by the CFI as soon as I landed. But I got away with it.

The weather was getting more and more black flag quality as the days grew shorter and the cloud base lower. The nearest we got to flying anything on most days now was the Link and even this came to an end when we had completed the mandatory course of twenty hours. My final efforts included 'flying' a Maltese Cross and then a Swastika, both being drawn on the table by the crab and showing excellent finishes joining up perfectly with the starts in each case. On the last exercise of all I 'flew' my name - Berry - only too thankful I was not called Featherstonehaugh! I scored an 'above average' for the course.

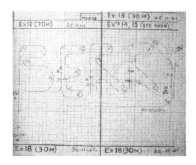

The Link Trainer print-out

One dual trip with PO Vaughan at this time enhanced my reputation very effectively. It was black and white flag weather with the cloud base down to below a thousand feet. Vaughan said, "We'll see if we can get through it and do some aerobatics." We took off and entered cloud as low as five or six hundred feet, much worse than anticipated. Vaughan carried on climbing however, on a compass heading and we finally broke cloud at three thousand feet. It was marvellous above that dense cloud carpet, brilliant dazzling sunshine as if reflected from a field of ice. We hadn't seen the sun for ages and we celebrated by doing a few slow rolls and stall turns and then Vaughan said we had better get back.

It was like diving into a dank grey soup as we entered the cloud again. Vaughan had control and he was flying back on the reciprocal of our climb up from the aerodrome. We scythed through the streaking mist with water streaming back from the struts and the windscreen as if going through torrential rain. The altimeter wound back past 1,000 feet, on down ... 800 ... 700 ... 600 ... 500 ... both of us peering intently over the side for signs of the ground. We got down to 200 feet and Vaughan was in the process of levelling out, not daring to go any lower without seeing something when we both glimpsed the dark shadows of trees whipping passed the trailing edge of the wings. It was a total clamp down, not safe for bats let alone aeroplanes!

Vaughan flew around for a bit and then his voice came over the Gosport, "Have you got your map with you Berry?" I confirmed I had. "Then see if you can plot where we are."

I looked down at the glimpses we were getting of roads, trees, fields and occasional houses through the dense mist, without making much sense of such fleeting references. It took me another five minutes to identify a sudden conjunction of road and railway lines. "I think I've got it," I shouted. "Good, give me a course for base."

I made a quick estimate and gave Vaughan a compass heading. He turned onto it, barely at treetop height it seemed.

"If I'm right we should be over Desford in about nine minutes." "You'd better be right or we'll miss supper," was Vaughan's only response as he struggled to keep the ground in view at a safe height.

About eight minutes later I shouted in relief, "Sir, there's Desford Church." We flew over the hangars on the perimeter seconds later and Vaughan sideslipped it down to land just in front of the dispersal. Flying had been washed out soon after we had taken off and we had long since been given up as missing as the fog descended. Vaughan said nothing as we walked in from the aeroplane.

CHAPTER 12

Because the weather was so unpromising from thereon we were given 48-hour passes for the following weekend and I just managed to catch the train down on the Friday evening. I told Joan to keep her fingers crossed as I hoped to get leave over Christmas. "That's the rumour anyway, but don't bank on it too much."

The startling news broke while I was at home that weekend of the Japanese attack on Pearl Harbour. Everyone seemed to think this was a good development in the long run though as it was bound to bring the Americans in. I took my bicycle back with me this time so that I could get back to camp before midnight from Leicester Station. I had nearly lost the last bus out to Desford twice now going back off leave and a third time could be disastrous!

We had an ENSA Concert that Tuesday, the highlight of which was 'The Shooting of Dan McGrew' by a very ham performer - not the most successful ENSA Concert I had ever seen. The earlier rumours about a posting were now seen as 'duff gen', because the latest news was that the course had been extended to 10th January.

We got some flying in most days thereafter, right through to Christmas Eve in fact, but with the hoped-for Christmas leave a non-event. There would be no flying on Christmas Day we were told - "Big Deal!" - and Christmas dinner would be duly celebrated in the Mess! In fact the way the Mess was being decorated and the general spirit that was developing was beginning to infect everyone and the whingeing began to die down as the day approached.

Two parcels arrived from home, one from Mum, containing a Christmas cake, mince pies, cigars, and stationery, and the other from Joan which included the book Fighter Pilot. This was a personal record of the Battle of France written by an anonymous Squadron Leader, anonymous because the book was published in wartime. Indeed, throughout the book Christian names only were used, which was unfortunate since it is a stirring account of the activities of a group of young RAF pilots fighting for their lives during the fall of France. Sir John Squire writing about the book in <u>The Illustrated London News</u> said, "The whole book is so decent and modest and brave and gay that it seems almost vulgar to mention the fact." It made a great impression upon me.

Christmas Dinner was scheduled for 1800 hours, the Mess having been put out of bounds from lunchtime onwards and when everyone arrived for the feast they found the Mess decorated with holly, streamers, balloons and coloured lights. The Mess Stewards and the Kitchen Staff had done a really splendid job, including white linen tablecloths and serviettes, bowls of biscuits on the tables with cheese, celery and bread. There were even printed menus which made unbelievable reading in this second year of war:

Crème Desford

Roast Turkey or Goose
Roast Beef
Roast Pork

Baked Potatoes
Boiled Potatoes
Brussels Sprouts
Apple Sauce

Christmas Pudding

Mince Pies
Cheese, Biscuits and Celery

To supplement the menu there were twenty free cigarettes for every man and as much free beer as anyone could drink. If we could not go home on leave for Christmas this was certainly an acceptable alternative! In accordance with tradition, all the Officers came in to wait on table and to serve the men.

"Double up there, I'm hungry ... Sir!" and to the Commanding Officer I heard "Take your thumb out of the soup!" PO Vaughan put a plate of soup down in front of me saying, "Make the most of this Berry, you'll never get another chance like it - you young bugger."

As if such a dinner were not enough in itself there was a running buffet all evening which included mince pies, sausage rolls, jam tarts, cakes, sandwiches, plus beer and minerals. While everyone got extremely merry the remarkable thing was that only a couple of the lads really over-indulged and actually got legless.

Boxing Day and it was all back to normal, flying in the morning and night flying scheduled for that night, indeed there was to be night flying for the rest of the week it seemed. I only got in one trip with PO Vaughan however, before flying was again washed out at 0100 by increasing winds gusting up to gale force. These winds did not abate for a couple of days, but by the 28th they had calmed sufficiently for night flying to be resumed. My first trip was with a PO Goggarty. There was nearly a full moon and visibility in the cold frosty night air was remarkably good. At 500 feet I could see the Hinckley Road, a pale grey ribbon between the darker patchwork of fields. It did not help with the actual landings though and one was still totally dependent upon the angle of the flare path for the hold off and touch down. After three good landings Goggarty sent me out to do a couple of circuits by myself.

It was a bitterly cold night and I was wearing everything I had available, including a woollen Balaclava beneath my helmet which Rene had knitted for me. After I had struggled into the cockpit, however, and had laboured to get the Sutton Harness secured, I was sweating cobs. It was always the same, if you got dressed too early you overheated like mad, and if you did not put enough on then you froze up in five minutes. I taxied out to the flare path, got a green Aldis and swung the plane out in between the lights. I found the take off quicker, the climb steeper and as with my first solo the aeroplane felt so much lighter and more responsive. It was astonishing how much difference it made with one body less in the plane. I climbed up to a thousand feet levelled out and turned on to the circuit. The blackout was complete, with not a glimmer of light anywhere away from the flare path. I decided that I enjoyed flying at night by myself immensely. There was an acute sense of remoteness and timelessness, just as if one had jumped worlds into another universe.

I had two more trips that night, the first a brief dual and the second flying solo. It was in fact to be the last bit of flying I would do for eleven days as the severe weather set in with a vengeance. The next morning the snow began to fall from a lead-heavy sky, camouflaging the airfield perfectly until it became indistinguishable from the rest of the landscape.

1942

The idleness enforced by the bad weather allowed us to listen to the Mess radio and to catch up on the war news, which was both good and bad. Although the Germans were being pushed back in the Crimean snows, the Japanese were advancing in the Pacific. News had come through on Christmas Day that Hong Kong had fallen after a seven-day battle, to be followed a few days later by the fall of Manila. The Japs it seemed were mounting a massive offensive in South East Asia. The island of Borneo was now occupied and they were advancing down the Thailand Peninsular to Singapore itself. The lads were not pleased by the news. It was one thing to contemplate an ultimate posting to Manston or Biggin Hill, but quite another to Burma!

"Let the Yanks fight that bloody war, we'll take care of Europe!" summed up everyone's feelings.

On the home front the main news concerned the lowering of the call-up age to $18^1/_2$ and the calling up of all women between the ages of 20 and 30 unless already engaged on work of national importance. Fortunately Joan's work in the Paper Mill, where they were making shell cases, was classified as work of national importance. It was a relief to turn the radio to programmes like ITMA and "Can I do you now Sir?" or even to the pedantry of Joad on the Brains Trust and to hear his catch phrase - "It all depends, Huxley, upon what you mean by creativity."

When flying was eventually resumed it was still bitterly cold and very misty with much of the snow persisting over the landscape. Map reading had to be re-learnt as all the familiar landmarks were now buried beneath the white blanket. It was a totally different countryside we were flying over. I wrote home to say that the Flight Commander, Flight Lieutenant Wynne-Powell, was taking an unusual amount of interest in my flying these days.

"The Flight Commander is giving me all my dual - paying me lots of attention lately. Either my flying is so good, or it's ruddy awful! He put me in the front seat today. It was like flying a different aeroplane. No one else has flown from the front. Is he going to put me up as an instructor??"

The last comment was meant to be a great funny, but the next day Wynne-Powell asked me, "If I give you a pupil and you take him up to do a cross country under the hood, do you think you'd get lost?" I promised I would not, enthused by the thought of flying one of my classmates and acting like an instructor in the front seat. "OK, I've got permission from the CFI for you to do this and I think you can cope. So, when the weather improves a bit I'll send you off." I was extremely 'chuffed' about this, as the locals would say, and I decided that the Flight Commander liked my flying after all.

It was at this time that I was put out into private billets sharing a room with George Thame in a semi-detached house at Leicester Forest East, on the fringe of Leicester. I had mixed feelings about this - not that the billet was anything but first class, but getting up at 0615 every morning to catch the 0700 transport into camp was not a benefit. The landlady, Mrs Smith, had four middle-aged daughters, one of whom, Alice, was paralysed from her neck down by polio. They were all gentle ladies straight out of a Jane Austen novel and the gentlest of them all was Alice. These five women completely spoilt we two airmen, feeding us and fussing over us like hens over their chicks. On the first Sunday after we had arrived, which happened to be a day off, we were brought breakfast in bed consisting of bacon, sausages, fried bread, butter and home made jam, all served on trays with white

94

doilies. For providing this service Mrs Smith was paid by the Royal Air Force - 6d per night, per person!

Another major benefit was that Leicester Forest East was only a 5d tram ride out of Leicester and of course, there was no need for late passes after a night out, not that either George or I were late birds used to going out on the town!

On the night of the 14th January there was a heavy fall of snow and when George and I arrived on camp the next morning we learnt that all the cadets on camp had been called out at 0300 to clear runways. This finally convinced me of the virtues of billeting out! The latest falls of snow with low cloud and fog persisted from the 17th to the 27th of January, with flying abandoned for the entire period. In spite of flying being so reduced by the bad weather, I had by now accumulated a total of 94.10 hours, which was nearly double what the course normally involved.

We did get in some sporadic flying during the first few days of February although the weather remained very severe. I then had a new experience as Duty Pilot for a day when I found myself sitting very importantly in the Watch Office in the Control Tower. My duties consisted of greeting all incoming visiting flights, checking the pilot's reasons for landing, along with his ultimate destination, and if in doubt reporting the landing to the CFI who lived in an office next to the Watch Office. Fortunately the traffic that day was sparse and I was saved the embarrassment of putting any suspicious visitors under an armed guard while I tried to find the CFI. I did get a kick, however, out of fraternising with the Squadron Leader who up to that time was very god-like and remote. Normally no cadet saw him until he had his final CFI's flight test and here he was sitting on my desk, swinging his legs, and making small talk about the traffic going on in the airfield outside the window.

It was while acting as Duty Pilot that I first heard the rumour about a posting on the 21st February. It came from a clerk in the Adjutant's Office who had brought something up for the CFI. "So, you should be off on the 21st then?"

"Off where?" I asked innocently.

"Oh, I don't know where. Burma I expect." And I could get nothing more out of him. I wrote home to Joan that evening:

"I haven't had my CFI's test yet, but there really does seem to be a possibility of me finishing up as an Instructor. PO Vaughan asked me casually how I'd like it and not putting any meaning to it, I said, "That wouldn't be a bad idea at all." (After all, he is an Instructor himself and I could hardly run the breed down). He then told me that if I showed the CFI on my test that I could fly accurately then I would probably be so recommended. Naturally I am very flattered to think that my flying is apparently good enough to warrant such a recommendation, but I have strong doubts about it. I have set my sights for so long on flying Spits and I'm getting so close to it now. I must find out how long an Instructor's tour lasts."

The rumour about a posting on the 21st was 'pukka'. The news came through on my birthday, the 17th, and there followed a great scramble to wind the course up. I finished with a grand total of 114.20 hours flying time, 46.30 dual and 59.35 solo day flying and 05.00 dual and 03.15 solo night flying. The assessments in my logbook were:

Proficiency as Pilot   -   *Above average*
Assessed as Ab Initio -   *Above average*

And additionally, but perhaps not surprisingly if Vaughan had anything at all to do with it:

Pilot Navigation   -   *Exceptional*

The initial posting for everyone was to the Pupil Pilots Pool at Peterborough from whence we would be posted to our ultimate Service Flying Training Schools. So, at this moment there was complete frustration, with no one knowing whether they were to be on fighters, bombers, Coastal Command, or what? The aim of the immediate exercise was obviously to clear everyone out from Desford to make room for the next intake.

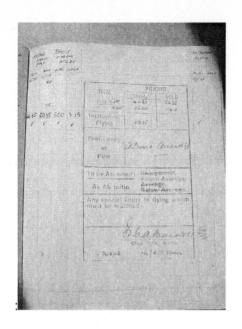

Log book entry, February 1942

CHAPTER 13

There were twenty-three airmen posted on to Peterborough out of the original fifty who started the course at Desford. Our numbers were sufficient to warrant transport, so we were saved the tedium of being shunted across country by train. We arrived on the Saturday afternoon to find RAF Westwood a very large, well-established, pre-war camp with a small landing field. First impressions, however, were not good. For a start, Peterborough itself looked industrial and unlovely and the camp, like any pre-war RAF station, looked well-used, tired and in need of investment and modernising.

"Oh God, there's a war on after all," someone muttered.

The accommodation - sleeping, messing, administration and so on - was all in a series of wooden huts. We were allocated to one of these, filling it exactly, to find iron beds with biscuits and blankets, just like ITW in fact, except that the environment was decidedly inferior. I had a fat, black, iron stove at the foot of the bed I selected belching out heat from its glowing belly. "At least I'll be warm," I decided. The ablutions were in a brick hut a couple of blocks away with a long line of basins down the middle and a concrete floor which streamed with water. This is how we feared all service life would be like. God, how we had been spoilt at Desford!

Dinner that evening however, went a long way towards ameliorating the earlier impressions. It was ample, tasty and well served. "Perhaps we can survive this place after all." I caught a bus into town after dinner, which was only a few miles in from Westwood, but apart from seven cinemas I found it didn't have much else to offer.

There would be some flying, we were told, while waiting for a posting, but it would only be a means of killing time rather than doing anything constructive. We were also promised some leave. I went across to the Administration Block next morning to see if I could find out anything about it. There were a few civilian girls working in the admin and one could not help noticing a particularly attractive young blond with a super figure. She appeared to have noticed me too. It is strange how one can tell these things, something to do with Darwin I expect! There was no firm news about leave, however, other than that if it did come through it would be soon.

Peterborough was a very boring place and we were only too thankful that the food at least was good. I decided to go in to the pictures that evening by way of escape. I was aware of sitting down next to a girl, but it was not until the lights went up in the interval that - surprise, surprise - it was the blond from the Admin Block! The chemistry immediately started building, along with my pulse rate, as I became acutely aware of her presence. I was hardly conscious of the film at this stage and then when I felt her foot pressing up against mine I completely lost all interest - in the film that is. A few minutes later and I had my leg touching hers ... she didn't pull back but returned the pressure. I moved my knee slowly, savouring the sensations I was getting, willing my hand to touch her knee ... her fingers light on the back of my hand, encouraging ...

For an endless time we sat there revelling in the dozy sexiness I, for one, was feeling, when she broke the spell. "I have to go now," she whispered," squeezing past me out to the aisle. The unbelievable thing was that I carried on sitting there, not following her! That I was supposed to get up and follow her out was in **CAPS** in the script. It seems though that it must have been one of the classics I had missed. A physical inertia froze me to my seat. She'd be miles away by now, I'd never catch her - but the sexual high was overwhelming. I would have missed the last bus back to camp though. Not good. Perhaps I could look her up in the admin office tomorrow? ... Somehow I knew I wouldn't! My mind buzzed with conflicting emotions not least of which was - feeling relieved. "God, what a wimp," I thought.

Next morning DROs (Daily Routine Orders), announced the great news that there would be 14 days leave as from Tuesday the 24th - passes and travel warrants to be collected immediately! It was a marvellous leave, the longest I had enjoyed in the eight months since 'Arcy Darcy'. It was long enough to take stock, long enough to talk about the future instead of watching the clock all the time and of being afraid of wasting a precious second. Plans for the wedding featured of course, but so did plans for what might happen afterwards.

"How terrific it would be if you could come and live near where I'm finally posted. Would you do that?" Joan nodded emphatically.

"Of course, it would depend entirely upon where I'm posted and what I'm posted on to do. As long as it's in this country it should be OK." "I'd have to get work of national importance, like with a firm making munitions, or something." "You could join the Land Army." "Like hell I could. I'd sooner join the WRENS." "Mmm ... I could fancy you in black stockings," which earned a momentary frown of disapproval.

"And what about after the war, Dennis, we've never talked about it?"

"I still want to be an architect, although God only knows how. I wouldn't mind carrying on flying either and I suppose I'd stand more chance at that than with architecture. What do you think?"

"I think we keep the options open. You'd make a good architect though, you love drawing - and it's much safer than flying." I thought about this for awhile, luxuriating in the notion of having a choice of professions and then frowning, I said, "Let's hope there's still some sort of world left to work in after this bloody war!" Joan snuggled up to me reassuringly.

A big excitement during the leave was deciding to buy a motorcar. The mobility it could provide would be enormously useful. Just having my bicycle on the station had demonstrated this, but to have a car would be so much more flexible. The petrol ration was awful but surely the extra gallon or so should be possible between the RAF and EGP Limited?

I spoke to Ern about it, about buying a car that is, not about black-market petrol. He said he had just the thing. I visualised a modern sporty looking vehicle, not costing too much of course. Ernest showed me a 1934 Morris 10/4, ten horse power and four cylinders. I was disappointed. This solid looking eight-year-old saloon was not quite the image I'd had in mind. Ernest agreed.

"Yes, it is a bit dull for you I suppose. Well, I'll leave you with it," and he walked away.

The car was really in splendid condition, not a mark on it, the tyres were all sound and the black leather upholstery looked as new. It really was quite a bargain at £30. I brought Joan down to see it and she thought it was marvellous.

I hadn't got a driving licence and in fact I'd never driven a car before, never that is other than Reg Fenner's Riley Alpine. Reg was a friend of brother Vic and I had only driven his car around the block when I was fourteen years old and without Reg's permission. I had stalled it on the hill, had walked back in great fear to tell Reg, who had then explained to me how to do a hill start and told me to go and fetch his ... car back - which I did!

So, back to the Morris 10/4 and I told my brother-in-law I wanted to buy it.

"Not so fast. Not before you've driven it anyway," and he took me out on a trip across to Maidstone, letting me drive it all the way. It all went fine, with Ernest even pretending to drop off to sleep. Then suddenly, coasting down the other side of Detling Hill, the car started to swerve from one side of the road to the other with me frantically oversteering to recover control. Ernest woke up very quickly and grabbed the wheel telling me to stop the car. We changed seats and Ernest tested the steering carefully. It was quite alright he found, I had simply got positive feedback on the steering and had overcorrected.

I bought the car and Ernest gave me a full tank of petrol to go with it. There was of course, no point in taking it back to Peterborough and having it with me until I knew where I was to be posted. But it was a great thrill to own my first motorcar. Its number plate was of great significance too - BUL 39 - as if there wasn't enough bull in the Air Force already!

Back at Peterborough, the anti-climax after such a wonderful leave was acute. There was still no news of a posting and not much flying to be had either. The day after I got back I had a brief flight with a Pilot Officer Donan who took me up to check out my landings and who then sent me off for an hour to fly around and to learn the local countryside. It was a relief to be flying once again and to look at Peterborough from the air. The railway branched in from the north in between the airfield and the town and then ran arrow-straight due south. It would be difficult to lose oneself I decided. The countryside to the northeast was pretty flat and dull right the way out to the Wash. I had another four solo trips during the next week to explore the surroundings, plus an hour's dual one night, which all served to keep me sane.

Then at last the postings came up on DROs. Most of the twentythree who arrived at Peterborough were going on to fly twins - Ansons and Oxfords - and only five were going on to fly singles, that is Miles Masters, at SFTS. I was posted to No 5 Flying Instructors' School at Perth, the only one out of the whole flight of fifty!

Now that the news was through and my suspicions confirmed, I felt bitterly envious of the five who were going on to fly Masters. I listened to their discussions about the merits and demerits of the Hurricane versus the Spitfire and envied their enthused anticipation. I asked for an appointment to see the Commanding Officer and surprisingly got one that afternoon. I marched into the great man's office, my speech prepared and rehearsed and snapped off a smart salute. The Wing Commander told me "At ease," and then greeted me with, "Congratulations Berry, I gather they're posting you to Instructors' School. Well done! Now what is it you want to see me about?"

I mentally tore up my prepared speech, gulped and plunged in. "Thank you Sir. It was about the posting I wanted to see you, Sir. Is it at all possible to have it changed? I really wanted to go on to fighters, Sir."

The Wing Commander nodded as if in sympathy. And then after a long pause, "Look here, I know you volunteered for fighters, but you have to remember that as a pilot you represent one man against the enemy. As an Instructor you will represent 20 men - 20 pilots in one year - against the enemy. This is the best way you can help us fight this war." He looked long and seriously at me and then nodded. "OK lad, off you go and - good luck."

"It's my own fault, I shouldn't have been so bloody clever!" I thought as I marched out of the office.

It was a bad journey up from Peterborough to Scotland. The train was packed solid and chuffed fussily along all night. The blackout permitted only the merest glimmer of lighting so that all one could do was sleep. I laid for three hours in the smoky corridor, using my respirator as a pillow, but what with the condensation dripping down from the windows on to my face and the constant traffic along the corridor to the loo, there was little hope of sleep. Inevitably I brooded upon the posting. In one sense I was flattered by the vote of confidence in my flying, but in another I felt cheated. I had not joined to fly Tiger Moths for the rest of the war, but on the other hand the prospect of being a Flying Instructor certainly fed my ego. I thought of how everyone had idolised their Instructor, how I had looked up to Vaughan as if he were the incarnation of D'Artagnan himself. The notion of having my own pupils looking at me like that was quite appealing. But as a child the image of the Hawker Fury, that gleaming silver biplane, the RAF's front line fighter, had always teased my imagination beyond measure. I had dreamed of one day being able to fly it, a dream that had then been updated by the appearance of the magical Hurricane. And now, just as I was so close to realising that dream, I was being cheated. It seemed very unfair. My resentment was not born out of any sense of frustrated heroism, for this aspect of flying and fighting had not really occurred to me as yet. I was still young enough not to question whether I would survive the war. Then I tried telling myself that the Instructor's Course would make me a far better pilot and by the time I got on to Spits I'd really know how to fly. I did not realise at that time that I could learn how to fly too well for fighting.

At about 0100, I finally managed to get a seat and wedged between two bodies dozed fitfully for the rest of the night. We arrived in Perth at 1100, having admired the engineering of the Forth Bridge through the mist. Perth itself also looked impressive, a large town with its busy shopping centre and river location.

Transport was waiting at the station for me and a couple of other RAF lads to take us out to the camp five miles north of Perth. By now the morning mist had lifted and I could see the rugged countryside of fir trees and bracken with, in the distance, what looked like snow tipped hills, or even low mountains. For a 'Townie' who until the war had never been further from London than Eastbourne the sight was very impressive.

We eventually turned off the main road and climbed about a quarter of a mile up to the aerodrome. At first sight I experienced once again the shock of the vast uninterrupted space which all airfields invoke, but this time with a difference, the dark looming hills beyond the perimeter if anything added to the sense of vastness and the air itself was bitingly fresh and exhilarating. If the impact of the aerodrome and its environment were stimulating, the wooden hut I was directed to as my quarters was not. It was certainly cleaner and newer than the Peterborough version but not up to Desford standards.

The new intake to the course, which comprised eleven others in addition to me, was addressed the following afternoon by the Commanding Officer, Squadron Leader Mason. The course was expected to last eight weeks and if completed satisfactorily, as at the end of the comparable SFTS, would carry with it the award of the Pilot's Brevet, the coveted 'Wings'. In addition we were told to expect our promotion to the rank of Acting Sergeant within the next two weeks. This came as a very pleasant surprise as it had been assumed that such promotion would not come through until we were awarded our Wings. We were told to report for flying at 0900 the following morning.

I had little idea as to what to expect from the course, but when we were issued with what they called the Instructor's Patter Book, a slim hard back, like a small diary, and told that we would be learning it word for word over the next eight weeks, I began to get the idea. My Instructor, Pilot Officer Carr-Lewty, turned out to be a small, beaky and at that first acquaintance, humourless man with whom I felt little immediate rapport. He took me up for a long trip, firstly to look at the countryside, secondly to sample my flying ability and finally to initiate me into the Instructor's Patter!

Although the weather was warm and sunny, more like mid-summer than early spring, I actually felt very unwell, flushed, but with cold shivers. I called into the Sick Bay after lunch and found that I had a temperature of 103. They put me straight to bed, dosing me up with the new wonder drug - M and B 693. The service was marvellous, the Medical Officer and the Orderlies were kindness personified. One of them kept renewing cold vinegar packs to my forehead during that night which I felt I could have done without as he kept waking me up to do it.

I had lots of visitors, the first the following evening greeting me with, "Hallo Sergeant Berry, how do you feel, you scrounger?" This was how I learned of the promotion which had just been confirmed. They brought me my stripes into the Sick Bay so that I was able to sew them on to my Battle Dress as I lay in bed. "Don't forget to use the Sergeants' Mess when you get out of here!"

I resumed normal duties on the 2nd April, having lost a week of flying. I had an hour and a quarter with PO Carr-Lewty and then went up with a couple of the other pupils to practise our patter. This seemed to be the pattern of the course, co-ordinating the flying demonstration of a given manoeuvre as smoothly as possible with its explanation. It assumed a fair mastery of flying the Tiger, that is flying by reflex rather than having to think about it, because fitting in the prescribed patter was a totally new skill to acquire.

I was not comfortable with the technique at all, it seemed very artificial and I was constantly wanting to extemporise, to exploit any incident which occurred to make the exercise more spontaneous. This was absolutely discouraged however, and I began to develop a lurking resentment about the course and about its illogicality. Much of this feeling of irritation was due no doubt to the fact that I was now a week behind the others and correspondingly behind with the patter. I tried very hard to rationalise my feelings, telling myself that this was how the entire Air Force had learnt to fly and how I had been taught and that it had all been worked out by people more clever than me. I broached my worry with my Instructor who perhaps dismissed it too briefly.

"It's a thoroughly tried and tested method. The patter's concise and to the point. And once you've done your demonstration you're free to advise your pupil on his efforts using your own words. But always remember - in the air, keep it simple - just like the patter." So I had to come to terms with the system and to make the best of it.

I was certainly only too happy to make the best of the new messing arrangements and it was something of a revelation to discover how the senior NCOs lived, dining off white tablecloths and being waited upon at table amidst the generally formal atmosphere stiffly maintained by the President of the Mess. This elderly Station Warrant Officer had little time for the Course Sergeants and tolerated them only as long as they did not disturb the routine of his Mess. I kept a very low profile for the first few days while I learned about Mess protocol.

Although a typical Training Command Station in the sense of tight organisation and formality, Perth was still a very happy posting. Learning to become a Flying Instructor proved to be an intensive and exacting activity, but apart from that, bull was at a minimum with no formal parades, inspections, or harassments of any kind. A Ground Defence Aircraftsman came in every day to sweep the hut, make the beds, light the fires and to tidy up generally. The food was very good and the nightlife in town satisfactory. I was constantly amazed by the Scottish hospitality I received from the locals, who treated the RAF with so much warmth and friendliness. This was not the case with the Poles however, who were also stationed in Perth and about whom the locals felt very differently. This had something to do with the way the Poles pursued the local girls - even harder than the RAF apparently.

Flying over the Scottish countryside was a marvellous experience. The airfield is in a valley with Perth about five miles to the south and the River Tay running down from the north, looping through Perth and then swinging back north east into the Firth of Tay and out to sea. At its widest, just west of Dundee, the Firth is about three miles across, the widest stretch of water I had ever flown over. To the west of the airfield the countryside becomes more and more undulating, rising eventually up to three and four thousand feet of a snow-capped and streaked range of hills, a very inhospitable-looking environment. To the east, another range of hills separates Perth from the sea and at a height of about 6,000 feet I could sometimes see the gleam of the water.

There was a constant strong wind blowing from the south west and, what with that and the undulating ground, flying was extremely bumpy even at the best of times making accurate flying that much more difficult.

About a quarter of the air time which I put in at Perth was on the Miles Magister, a low wing monoplane equipped with dual controls in tandem, like the Tiger Moth. Although with a fixed undercarriage, the Magister had Bendix brakes operated by a hand lever on the control column which made taxiing that much easier - and safer. It was also equipped with vacuum operated flaps. The power plant was the same as in the Tiger Moth, the 130 hp De Havilland Gipsy Major four cylinder in-line inverted air-cooled engine, but in the Magister it gave a top speed of 145 mph, as against the 109 mph of the Tiger Moth.

The Magister was a delightful aeroplane to fly, with characteristics not dissimilar from the Tiger Moth, but without the top wing of the Moth it obviously had much better visibility overhead. The spin was a bit sharper but recovery just as easy. My first reaction was that there was much less aeroplane to relate visually with the horizon, but this did not prove to be any sort of handicap in flying straight and level, nor in aerobatics. Indeed, it was a much easier aeroplane to trim and aesthetically more satisfactory with its cleaner and less cluttered shape. Like the Tiger Moth, the Magister was also equipped with the blind flying hood for instrument flying. It was under the hood in a Magister that I was first required to spin and recover - on instruments. The spin sensation under the hood was totally disorienting with every instrument on the panel in front of me going haywire. The Turn and Bank Indicator gave a full right turn and a full left skid - something I had never seen before; the Altimeter was unwinding with frightening speed and the ASI was climbing alarmingly. The recovery, when it came, while registering on the instruments with the Turn and Bank Indicator centralising, was definitely not registering on me. My head carried on spinning furiously and I had to force myself to disregard these sensations and to rely upon the instruments. That, of course, was the objective of the exercise.

While flying from Perth there was an ever-present hazard of the weather closing down and the cloud base descending below the hilltops. If this happened while over the high country one had to scuttle back to the airfield down a convenient valley before the cloud base reached ground level. This did happen to me on one occasion and I was nearly caught out by the rapidity with which the weather deteriorated. I had been flying over in the region of Loch Tay when the cloud had started to come down and I wisely set course for base. Some of the hilltops reached over 2,500 feet in that area and the cloud was already below 2,000 feet. I was in sight of the River Almond between the Meall Tarsuin spot height at over 2,600 feet and Ben Chonzie at above 3,000 feet, both already lost in cloud. I followed the stream and the road eastwards looking ahead constantly for likely fields I could use if the weather clamped right down. No way could I dare lose sight of the ground. The cloud base was now down to below 400 feet and totally obscuring the tops of the hills either side so that I was now flying along a winding tunnel which the valley had become. The light had diminished and in the near night-gloom visibility was extremely poor, so that flying at 80 miles an hour within a few feet of the ground was quite hairy with things like trees happening very suddenly.

By the time I emerged, sweating heavily, from the valley and had picked up the Pitlochry road the cloud base was right down on the deck. Slipping over the perimeter fence I crept into the airfield offering up a grateful prayer as my wheels trundled thankfully over the grass.

I flew and worked hard for the next four weeks, my flying becoming more and more crisp in response to the ever-demanding Carr-Lewty. But on the 6th May misfortune struck again in the shape of acute lumbago. I woke up to find I couldn't stand, or straighten my back, without great pain. I hobbled to the Sick Bay once more and received forty minutes of infrared heat and then a large pad of thermogene was strapped round my middle and I was sent back to rest on my bed. After a few minutes of this the thermogene began to heat up nicely and to heat up ... and to heat up ... and heat up ... and up ... until I was in far worse pain than originally. By the time I had got back to the Sick Bay the pain was a real burning sensation. They took the strapping off and found I had indeed a grade A burn about a foot square on my back. My lumbago, however, was quite cured!

I lost three more days flying over this incident and even when I resumed I was very uncomfortable for days, chafing beneath the Sutton Harness.

The Ground Exams loomed and necessitated heavy swotting during the previous week. Everyone had found the lecture courses quite demanding and, as ever, a gloomy few predicted failure but in the event everyone passed. The final exam, the 'Wings' Exam, was the Flight Test with the Chief Flying Instructor and these started on Wednesday 13th May. Half a dozen of the pupils were tested on that day and all were successful. That evening, their newly-sewn-on 'Wings' were properly baptised in the Mess and even the dour old Mess President helped to 'wet' them with an appropriate quantity of ale. After that first batch of testing nothing more happened for a week and morale slumped generally.

I wrote home: "I'm feeling very unsettled and restless. I haven't had my test yet and I feel very irked about it. It is a so-and-so nuisance. They tested six of the boys last Wednesday and they're all walking about with their wings up – fully-fledged Sergeant/Pilots - with smug grins all over their silly faces! Then for some reason they stopped testing any more until Sunday - tomorrow. Having got this far it is so frustrating to have to wait about like this."

And I did have to wait in fact until the following Wednesday when I was finally called out to fly with Flight Lieutenant Swanston, the CFI, a doyen from the Empire Flying Training School at Hullavington. The test lasted an hour and a quarter and ranged over the full flying syllabus. It was a clear, bright, but very windy day and the bumpy conditions were not good for accurate flying. I gave it every ounce of concentration I could muster, responding carefully to the requests to demonstrate this or that manoeuvre. The poor flying conditions probably acted in my favour as I had to concentrate more on my flying than on the patter which, as a result, came out more naturally than it normally did.

Whatever the influences, I passed. I joined the rest of the course that evening sewing my 'Wings' on to my battle dress and tunic. This was the proudest day of my life! Nothing I ever did after that quite equalled it, not even my success in the architecture exams and appointment as an Associate of the Royal Institute of British Architects.

Daily Routine Orders the next day completed the story with the announcement that

> *Sgt/Pilot Dennis Berry posted w.e.f 29 May 1942*
> *to No 7 EFTS RAF Desford, to report for duty*
> *12 June 1942. 14 days leave pass and travel warrant*
> *now available in the Orderly Room.*

I collected my Log Book with my leave pass and travel warrant to find it stamped and signed - *Provisionally Qualified to Carry Out Ab Initio Instruction.*

An insert, Form 414 (A), further attested to the assessment of my ability ...

> *As a L/AC Pilot Instructor   Average C*

I could have done better!

CHAPTER 14

All the other weddings I had ever experienced, like those of my two sisters and my brother, had been grand family affairs, attended mostly by relatives only ever seen at such events - or at funerals - and maybe at Christmas. Perhaps my childhood recollections were over-drawn, but in my memory all the women wore bright new hats and all the men, like identical penguins in their Moss Bros. gear, would greet each other noisily - "Hullo 'So-and-So' how are you? You look so well. How is 'So-and-So'? ... Oh, I had not heard! Did she suffer? ... I'm so sorry. But you do look well." The tables spread with silver, the to-ing and fro-ing animating the scene and all was excitement and unusual, like birthday time for a seven year old.

Sittingbourne, 1942

But this wedding in 1942 was not like those others. It was quiet and there were no noisy distant relatives rediscovering each other. There were very few people there at all in fact, just the immediate families.

Joan wore white, looking very serious and attractive, I wore my best blue embellished with the white and gold wings and the pale blue stripes. The recently imposed ban by the government on embroidery on women's underclothes and nightdresses had no significance for us. Joan's wardrobe was simple as befitted a wedding in wartime. We were very proud of each other and the sun shone and the families were very happy for us.

We drove away that afternoon in the new car to Devon for the honeymoon, staying as the only guests on a farm near Kingsbridge, where we did very little apart from looking at the cows and eating and pleasing each other. The war for a week was elsewhere - on another planet.

Now as Sergeant/Pilot Dennis Berry, I reported to the Chief Flying Instructor at Desford on my first Instructor's posting and was greeted jovially enough by the Squadron Leader. "I thought we had seen the last of you."

"They couldn't keep me away Sir. The ... er ... food's too good."

Wardell asked his deputy, Flight Lieutenant Brett to give me a test flight, after which I was told to report to the Officer Commanding B Flight, Flight Lieutenant Brookes. After that and a few further interviews, including one with the Adjutant, and I reckoned I was on the establishment. It was all a bit different when as a mere LAC Pupil Pilot I had first arrived at Desford. Now, with my new status and the friendly reception it received everywhere, I felt on top of the world.

Even though I was allocated to a bed unit similar to the one I had occupied as an LAC Cadet, it was still the best accommodation I had experienced in the Air Force to date and I was more than content. I drove out that evening to see my old landlady, Mrs Smith, and her daughters, who made a great fuss of me. "Come in and see Alice," and Alice fluttered her deathly white hand at me with a "Coo," of real delight. They suggested I called on a Mrs Davey, who they knew was thinking about letting a flat. Mrs Davey had a semi-d around the corner from the Smith family in Park Drive and she turned out to be a divorcee with a young son of about 9 years of age and a fat, friendly cocker spaniel called Prince. Yes, she had a flat to let - bedroom, sitting room, use of kitchen and bathroom - and at a reasonable price too. She was quite a character, I decided, sharp to the point of shrillness almost, extremely thin and with pebble glasses which made her peer at everything with off-putting intensity.

"They say that two women in the same kitchen is a disaster, but I'm sure we can work to a timetable, or something," she said staring hard at me and nodding aggressively. "Oh yes and the bathroom too. We'll have a roster for that."

If her mien was unpromising there was something about her which made me want to laugh - not at her, but at her attitude and at what she said. She was so down to earth and normal. The Smiths had said she was a lovely person and very kind. The flat was well furnished and I could not imagine getting anything better so I took it as from the following month. It turned out to be the happiest choice possible. Mrs Davey and Joan got along famously, with Mrs Davey teaching Joan how to cook and giving her, in passing, the marriage wisdom of the world - not all of which Joan told me about! Young Micky Davey brought his model aeroplane problems to me and I was reminded in the process of my own relationship with my brother-in-law Ron. Mrs Davey told Joan "He's a born teacher, that man."

Joan got a job in Leicester as a secretary to an accountant and went off to catch the 8.30 bus in the morning at the same time that I left in the car for the airfield. It was a very happy time for us, even if the war news was less than encouraging. The Japs had already taken Mandalay and there was now news of their submarines raiding Sydney Harbour as well as shelling Sydney and Newcastle. 10,000 US and Filipino troops had surrendered in Corregidor and it seemed that as fast as we sat on the enemy in Europe so the other enemy in the Far East made advances. The nightmare of a posting to Burma persisted to haunt the dreams of everyone in the Mess, for the reports of the Japanese atrocities committed in the jungle theatre were commonplace. The news that someone called Harris had taken over Bomber Command and that he was on record as having said, "We will scourge the 3rd Reich from end to end," cheered the lads enormously.

The first 1,000-bomber raid on Cologne was taken as evidence that he meant it too.

"Thank Christ someone is having a bash at them after all the poor sods in London have had to take."

"And you can also thank Him that you're not flying one of Harris's Lancs. That must be one hell of a picnic." The others agreed with this. "I'll stick with my Tiger, if I may." This last comment struck me as quite unusual. It was not the normal sentiment one heard in the mess. "Perhaps things are changing. We are too comfortable here," and I began to feel pangs of guilt.

A scheme had been started about this time to allow flying instructors to join the crew of a bomber on a mission over Germany. It was thought up no doubt by some otherwise intelligent twit in Flying Training Command to boost the morale of the poor frustrated instructors and to give them a piece of the action. The idea was not very popular though, except perhaps with the retarded and those of limited imagination. Most of the instructors, including me, were after all frustrated fighter pilots and the notion of going along as ballast in the rear seat of a Lancaster to stooge over Berlin appealed not one bit. I was not aware of a single application going forward from the station to join a bomber mission. So, Command made it compulsory - 'You *will* have your morale boosted ...'.

Fortunately, there were very few such postings and the few that did come through left the recipients chastened and very quiet about their experience. No one envied the bomber boys these days. I thought of the role of flying a bomber as being like an unarmed taxi driver in the rush hour at whom every one wants to shoot - and ultimately is bound to hit! "If it has to be bombers eventually, let it be Mosquitoes. Now there's a real fighter!" No one disagreed with this.

Those first few months in my new career as a flying instructor were a bit awesome. With only a bare two hundred hours of flying time in my logbook, here I was posing as the expert in front of my pupils. Not that any of them would have noticed whether I had two hundred or two thousand hours, however, they were all as bemused as I had been at that stage. The very first day I flew six trips with three pupils, a total of just under four hours. I felt absolutely exhausted that evening. It was obviously a tiring business, this instructing. I was enjoying it though; the actual flying, as well as the status the role seemed to carry.

It was all going along famously when, only a few weeks after I had started, I was literally brought down to earth with a bump - I had a flying accident from which I fortunately walked away. I had just got my pupil on to landings and was demonstrating a glide approach. Pattering away I brought the plane over the boundary at 65 miles an hour, prior to flaring out for the landing, when there was a stomach-lurching crunch and the plane seemed to falter in the air. I punched the throttle wide open and hauled the stick back. We had obviously hit something and I knew it had to be another aeroplane underneath us.

We wobbled along fifteen or so feet up gathering flying speed. It responded to the controls normally it seemed and I gingerly climbed a few more feet. From my position directly over the lower wings I could see nothing underneath the plane.

"I don't know if we still have an undercarriage. Can you see anything below us?" My pupil craned his head out as far as he could. "No Sir. I can't see anything."

"Lower your door flap and try again." I watched him in the mirror straining his head over the side, but the undercarriage was still out of his view beneath the wing – or was it simply missing!

I banked gently at the end of the field and flew back down the boundary towards the hangars. I could see a group of fitters and riggers standing there on the apron. I banked and circled directly over them, flying as low as I dared nearly on top of the hangar roof. I could see their white faces peering up, hands over their eyes, as they strained to inspect my aircraft. I quite expected to see someone holding up a wheel or something and was enormously relieved to see thumbs-up signals instead. "So far so good," I thought. "But this has to be a real daisy cutter," and I lined the plane up on the blood wagon and the fire tender which were now standing in the middle of the field waiting for us. I stalled the plane down on to the grass in probably the gentlest landing I'd ever made and it rolled to rest within feet of the blood wagon. Everything was intact. No damage at all.

I discovered later that I had landed on top of another plane, smashing its port wing completely, but fortunately without hurting its occupants. I was also very fortunate in not entangling my undercarriage in the process otherwise we could have arrived very suddenly - at sixty-five miles an hour - on the nose! "Just another inch or so lower..."

The sequel the following day happened when I was summoned to the C.O's office. Wearing my best blue with freshly polished brass I flung up my smartest parade ground salute and waited for the wrath of God to fall. The C.O was remarkably low key however.

"Please keep your head out of the 'office' in future and do not bend any more of my aeroplanes. Remember you aren't the only one entitled to airspace around here!"

I knew that I had learnt a very important lesson and one which served me well for the rest of the war. 'There are old pilots and there are bold pilots - but there aren't any old, bold pilots.' The old adage rang very true. One doesn't often get a second chance flying.

Getting a pupil off on his first solo was always a great moment. The casual "Off you go - one circuit only" from the flight commander belied the anxiety I always felt. As I watched the plane climb up and then turn onto the circuit I knew that I felt far more nervous than the lad up there in the cockpit. The entire airfield seemed to know when it was a first solo and that one lonely aeroplane, as it wobbled in over the perimeter, became the focus of attention. The first solos always went successfully though and it was usually a bit later that things would go wrong - if they were to go wrong, that is - which was not often. Very occasionally there would be a heavy landing, or a plane would finish up on its nose, or on its back, the shaken occupant hanging helplessly in his harness. More damage was done falling the two or three feet to the ground through releasing a harness without due care than in any other way. Much has been said and written about the forgiving nature of the old Tiger Moth. I swear it is all true. She was the sweetest and most forgiving aeroplane ever built.

My worst moment was when I sent a pupil off to practise circuits and landings for half an hour. After the first circuit the plane disappeared. Two hours later and there was still no sign of it. The Tiger's endurance with a full tank was only a little over two and a half hours and at the end of that time it had to come down wherever it was. My pupil only had a couple of hours solo and certainly no experience in forced landing procedures.

Just on the two and a half hours and there was a phone call. Great relief ... He had forced landed somewhere and was ringing from a nearby pub. He had got lost on the circuit - a mystery in itself as it was a perfectly clear day - had stooged around for a couple of hours trying to find the aerodrome and had finally given up and landed in a field. The Duty Officer was in the throes of congratulating him on a safe landing when the pupil told him of the name of the pub. It was the Red Cow, the local pub just half a mile from the airfield!

The final irony was when I arrived to fly the plane out. I found the field was barely big enough in which to swing a cat, let alone to land a plane. In fact the Tiger had to be dismantled and brought back by road.

I had only been in post for a couple of months when someone was required to go on a course and, being the newest recruit, I inevitably drew the short straw. It was called an Aircrew Refresher Course and consisted of two weeks of gruelling physical training, unarmed combat and dinghy drill in the local swimming baths. I discovered on arrival that the course started at eight o'clock every morning for the likes of me and at six o'clock for aircrew who were on the 'punishment' version of the course. Other than the two-hour earlier start the two courses, the normal and the punishment, were identical. The whole event came as a very harsh surprise to me. I thought I had risen above such treatment. Even the venue, a splendid hotel on the front at Brighton, was no amelioration for, as well as the curfew then in operation, the promenade itself was spiked with scaffold poles and laced with barbed wire. Indeed the war looked quite local sometimes when one could see convoys being dive-bombed out in the Channel.

I had softened up quite a bit since ITW and the fierce regime of exercise came very hard at first. But by the end of the second week I guess I was much fitter once more. I was very glad to get back to Desford again though and to its relative life of ease. My Flight Commander acknowledged my newly acquired skills by detailing me to take the rest of the Flight for PT on the Wednesday afternoon games periods. This I enjoyed hugely as, ignoring their groans, I sadistically rung the sweat from them.

It was not unheard of for one to borrow a Tiger and to fly home for a weekend and I got permission to do just this. The fighter airfield at Detling was only a few miles out from Sittingbourne and I got approval to enter 11 Group's airspace and for a landing. I also checked that they would be able to refuel me with 87 Octane and not the more potent 100 Octane introduced after the fall of France for the Merlins of the Hurricanes and Spitfires.

My fitter, a very large urbane 30 year old aptly called 'Tubby' Warner, asked if he could go along with me as he too had relatives in Kent.

It was a clear, bright midsummer's morning when, having picked Tubby up at the Braunston roundabout, I drove out to the aerodrome. It was useful having Tubby along with me, for with no flying on the Saturday morning I would otherwise have had difficulties in getting my plane off the pickets and started. One was not supposed to swing a propeller without having someone in the cockpit. It was possible to do this of course by strapping the stick back in the harness and running round to the cockpit as soon as the engine fired to throttle back. Tales are told, however, of unhappy airmen being chased across the airfield by pilotless aeroplanes.

We duly took off and set course for London. The climb up to 3,000 feet took an age and when I finally levelled out I found the cruising speed was just under seventy miles an hour and that with nearly full throttle. The plane felt sluggish and tail-heavy although the engine was giving normal power. Tubby was a big chap I knew, but surely not so big as to make all this difference. I was too embarrassed to mention the problem to him and setting the trimmer well forward I carried on with the flight.

We skirted London to avoid the balloon barrage, going well west over Maidenhead and then south over Reigate and Redhill. I flew on past Detling, down the London Road, losing height until we arrived over the house. We were down to about 500 feet as I started circling and then down to 300 or so feet. I could see everyone in the garden and identified my brother waving what must have been a large white tablecloth. I blipped the engine in response and then pulled up and away for Detling. I was not tempted to go much lower over the treetops as the plane felt so sluggish, even with full throttle, so I resisted the beat-up I had promised myself.

By the time we had landed, booked in and made our way to the guardroom and out to Detling Hill, my brother was waiting for us in his car. Everyone had been very thrilled by the low flying display over the house and they all made a great fuss of us. I didn't mention my worry about the performance of the aeroplane to the family, although Tubby did question the low cruising speed on the way down. Neither of us could account for it.

The return flight the next day nearly started with drama. Detling is quite a small airfield with a belt of tall trees on its western boundary, or they certainly looked like very tall trees to me as we raced towards them on the take-off run. The plane felt even more sluggish than it had on the flight down. We bounced from bump to bump across the grass with little sign of getting airborne, the trees on the boundary getting closer and closer. I was pushing the throttle up to its stop hard enough to push it right out of the cockpit. The wheels finally unstuck and I held it down as the trees rushed up, trying to build airspeed to clear them. At the very last moment I hauled the stick back and we wobbled over the treetops with just inches of clearance and the airspeed barely above stalling. There was no comment from the back seat and I wondered whether Tubby knew how close it had been.

I declared the aeroplane unserviceable when we got back and it was duly wheeled away into the hangar. Later a rigger reported on his inspection. "5695 Sarge. That kite couldn't fly. It was rigged with one degree of negative incidence on the top plane. No way could you have taken off, let alone fly it." "But George, I not only flew it, I had Tubby Warner in the back seat."

The rigger stared at me, his mouth slightly open. "Christ. It's a bloody miracle," he breathed.

CHAPTER 15

The news came through like a bombshell - a posting. I knew it was a mistake to get too settled. Desford was such a cushy number and to have all the home comforts of living-out with one's wife was unbelievably lucky. It made the news of a posting that much more miserable. The fact that it was said to be a temporary posting for three or four months only did not lessen the disaster. It was a catastrophe for us when I was given the five days notice to report on the 17th November to 28 Elementary Flying Training School, RAF Wolverhampton.

I had only just previously gained promotion on my Instructor's rating from the provisional C category, to B category, the normal one for instructors to hold. The rating above B was A2, but this would be a long way off - if ever achievable - as it was usually reserved for Flight Commanders, Chief Flying Instructors and the like. There must have been an A1 category, but I never heard of it – reserved for God, perhaps? I had been preparing for the recategorisation for weeks, having dummy test flights with my Flight Commander and finally with the CFI. A Flying Officer Jack from the Central Flying School at Hullavington had visited the station and had taken me up for the test. He took me through the whole syllabus, an hour and ten minutes of meticulous flying and patter and I presumably performed OK because he told me immediately we had landed that I had passed.

It was an amazing situation which had led to the unexpected posting. The two warring factions, the Allies and the Axis, were both courting neutral Turkey and both of them did a deal at the same time with that country to train some of their airmen. The first cohort of Turkish officers were due to arrive at Wolverhampton for three months ab initio training creating a need for more instructors there and I was one of those called for the occasion. RAF Wolverhampton was based on the Municipal Airport, an old pre-war aerodrome on the northern perimeter of the city. It was altogether a much larger station than Desford and long established. They flew Tiger Moths of course, but Boulton and Paul Defiants were also assembled at Wolverhampton and one often saw these unsuccessful and unloved aeroplanes on the circuit. The other notable circuit feature which astonished me when I first saw them was a pair of factory chimneys to the south of the airfield in the middle of Wolverhampton. They reared up almost to circuit height and in misty conditions were a very real hazard, so much so that the circuit would be changed from left handed to right handed, depending upon the wind direction, to avoid flying over them.

I was allocated to Flying Officer Teddy Hillman's C Flight which flew from the satellite field at Penkridge, about ten miles north of the parent aerodrome. This involved flying out every morning from Wolverhampton and back again in the evening, which was done with a pupil to save wasting time.

Joan had insisted that she should come with me even though it was only to be for a few months, but Mrs Davey was very unhappy at the thought of us giving up the flat in Park Drive and she readily agreed to us paying her a small retainer to keep it while we were away. I went out flat hunting every night in the first week of my arrival before I found somewhere half suitable and Joan moved over to Wolverhampton the following week. She immediately started looking for something better and we moved again a week later. These second digs served until Christmas when I had a seven-day leave and we went home to Kent.

Dad did not look well, his face was drawn and lacking its normal colour. "I hate him going out so early these mornings. He comes in and his fingers look bloodless, he gets so cold." Mum would never have said such a thing in front of Dad, who she looked upon as a great baby as far as health was concerned. "He's not a young man anymore."

I agreed with Mum but, in the habit of the family, put aside further consideration of Dad in favour of her health. She was the one we all thought of as delicate, the one to be cosseted. Dad was the tough one with hands of iron and a complexion like leather.

"He's alright Mum, but what about you? Are you still worrying about your baby, or have you finally realized that I can take care of myself?" She waved my question aside.

"I don't think I shall ever have peace of mind again. What with you and your Father and that poor Vie over there with that young boy. She worries the life out of me. Rene is the only one I can be sure of - and she can only do whatever He lets her do." 'He' being Ernest, of course.

It all sounded familiar enough to me. Things at home had obviously not changed. Joan's family made a great fuss of us, with old Mr Wyver sitting in his corner, not saying much, sucking his gums and clicking his plate of false teeth, nodding ponderously when someone said something he thought made sense, although this was not very often. He did approve of me though and I always thought he made a great deal of common sense, which the rest of his family did not.

1943

Going back off leave was a bit of a drama, arriving in Wolverhampton at dusk laden with luggage but no digs to go to. We called at five addresses without success and finished up at the police station where we were given a few more addresses. The best we could find, however, was a very sleazy boarding house where we got a bed for that night. In the absence of anything else Joan booked us into an expensive hotel the next day. The bed was sheer luxury after the previous night and the breakfast excellent. It did cost £1.1s.0d, but was worth every penny of it! Fortunately, one of the earlier contacts I made rang me at the station the next day with an address which turned out to be extremely suitable and we moved in that evening.

The Turks proved to be very amiable, immensely keen and enthusiastic. They were also quite fearless - foolishly so! As soon as they had gone solo, but were still very inexperienced, they would be seen dog-fighting each other and trying to aerobat and nearly falling out of the sky in the process. Sadly two of them did - and killed themselves - colliding at 3,000 feet. This quietened the rest of them down, but only for a bit.

123

I made great friends with another instructor in Teddy Hillman's Flight, a Sergeant called "Tubby" Wild. Tubby was an ex-railway engine driver, an enormous man who waddled rather than walked, his girth was so vast. His humour was lavatorial and excessive, as broad as his belly and everyone loved him. I would watch him in fascination as, red-faced, he would puff and squirm and wriggle to get his body down into the cockpit. "What you bleedin' laughin' at? These fuckin' seats are made for fuckin' midgets. I can't even fart in 'em..."

But Tubby could fly like an angel. It was a strange paradox that where this Falstaffian character had previously been driving enormous, smoke-belching, brutish monsters on steel rails, he was now capable of jinking this butterfly-like contraption so delicately on the wind. He was a man of great contrasts, he ate like a pig, but abhorred alcohol, he was obsessed by sex, but utterly faithful to his 'old woman' as he called his wife. It was his earthy honesty which appealed to me and his total lack of pretension.

"Them Turks are bloody crazy," he would say scratching his behind, "I hope we never have to fight 'em!"

No 28 Elementary Flying Training School
RAF Wolverhampton, 24th February 1943

124

The weather was bad and flying often curtailed by high wind and rain, but the Turks made good progress and by mid-January I had my four pupils on to aerobatics. Cross country flights followed to Sealand, near Liverpool, to Mier and I even took one over to Desford where my old Flight Commander, Flight Lieutenant Brookes, made me very welcome.

The Turkish course finally came to a successful end in February and the Turks invited the NCO instructors over to the Officers' Mess for a party. I wrote home: "They gave us one great hell of a time. I was surrounded by my four pupils the entire evening and never without a full glass in my hand and a cigarette in my mouth. One of them gave me a box of cigars and collectively they gave me a photograph of the Flight signed on the back - From Mahmet Ersin, Ali Baydar, Ismail Iscimen and M Sen, to our Flying Instructor Sergeant Berry."

I was very pleased by their genuine warmth, especially so when Lt. Iscimen, before leaving the station, came over to the Sergeants' Mess again to thank me for all I had done for them.

CHAPTER 16

We returned to Desford just before Easter when Mrs Davey was away and we had the house to ourselves. Unfortunately, I was Duty Officer on the Easter Sunday which ruined the brief holiday for us. While we had been away, "B" Flight had moved out to the satellite field at Braunston which was disgustingly convenient for me as it was only a mile away from the flat. The other major virtue was that Braunston operated as a self-contained unit with its own refectory, Sick Bay, hangar and maintenance personnel. The Flight of cadet pilots were housed on site and 'bussed' over to Desford daily for lectures. The Flight Commander, Flight Lieutenant Brookes, was also the station CO and life was altogether extremely pleasant for everyone.

The restoration of our comfortable lifestyle, however, was curiously unsettling, particularly after the shock of the surprise posting to Wolverhampton. "You mustn't lose sight of the possibility of a posting on to ops you know." Joan looked up at me quickly. "I know. Have you heard something?" "No, it's OK. I'm just saying it can happen though. Steve Warren was posted to AFU while we were away." "But you've only been instructing for about eight months and Steve was here for years." "Well, I didn't anticipate more than a year on this lark."

Joan looked at me very hard. "Do you want a posting to ops?" I didn't answer. "Dennis, do you still want to fly on operations?" I shook my head.

"No, I guess not, to be honest. This is what worries me. We are far too happy and comfortable here and it cannot last, Joan. It isn't what I joined for and when it does come - it's going to be bloody." "So - it will be bloody, but let's enjoy what we've got while we've got it." She put her arm around my shoulder. "Come on darling. Sufficient unto the day – and all that."

As the spring of 1943 progressed so the flying intensified. With the Allies beginning to step up their air offensive, the demand for more and more bomber crews mounted and the pressure began to increase on the flying schools. The message came down to the Flights from the CFI that everyone was expected to get in five hours a day instructing. At my level, that is without a strategic view of the war, the call for more flying was always received with some scepticism, if not cynicism. The commercial involvement of the company which owned the airfield with the number of hours flown was unjustifiably suspected by the instructors and any call to increase flying time therefore tended to be viewed with suspicion. The reality soon became apparent, however, as the bomber offensive increased. The 900 tons of bombs dropped on Berlin in one raid in March, the heaviest up to that time, had increased in just two months to 2,000 tons dropped on Dortmund.

Sergeants' Mess, RAF Desford, 1943

In that March I did 56 hours instructing, a normal amount for the month, but by June this total was doubled to well over 100 hours and these sorts of averages were then maintained for the rest of the summer. To exceed 100 hours a month meant that on the available flying days well over 5 hours a day instructing were necessary and as much of this time was spent on circuits and landings it meant the instructor's nerves were screwed up about fifty times each day with the pupil trying to kill them both, to say nothing of the hazards of sitting there while he tried to get out of a spin, or hanging inverted as he put on negative G at the top of a loop, and so on, and so on...

I found, along with most of the instructors, that I could take just so much, but when that point was exceeded I was in danger of screaming with impatient frustration. Above everything else, patience was the prime requisite and it was useless shouting at some terrified erk in the back seat because he couldn't get it together. Perhaps I was just a poor instructor. It is a fact that no one gave me an AFC for flying my heart out, which many of my colleagues received.

Anyway, I did succumb once to the strain and this was after a particularly intensive period of flying. My pupil was nearly there, but missing a neat landing each time by a whisker. Again and again I corrected him, but each time without effect. It was the end of a long hot day, I was very tired and my nerves must have strung to breaking. I banged the throttle open just catching the Tiger at the point of stall, ten feet too high and powered it down to earth. I felt like murdering the 'idiot' in the back seat. It was all too impossible. I taxied over to the apron at near take-off speed, slammed my doors down, flung the Sutton Harness straps back over my shoulders, climbed out and without a word to the pupil, leaving my parachute on the grass, ran over to the Sick Bay.

"For Christ's sake ground me." And I think I stood there blubbering.

I was off for three days and then back on full flying duties once more. Considering the hours flown it was amazing there were so few casualties. One particularly sad death however, was that of Terry Alderdyce who only a few weeks earlier had married, amidst great celebration, one of the girls in the Motor Pool. He was an extremely experienced pilot and yet he crashed in a field away from the aerodrome while flying solo. No explanation was ever found for the cause of the crash and, as I was known as a keen photographer, I was ordered by the CO to go out and photograph what was left of the crashed aeroplane. Not a pleasant assignment.

Not all accidents were so tragic and most ended up with broken aeroplanes rather than bones. Lt. Jeffries was a Lieutenant on secondment from the army, who had previously been flying Austers on army reconnaissance. Just why he should be have been seconded to the air force as an instructor was a mystery to everyone and mostly to him. I suppose it was down to the urgent need for more pilots at that time. He went very overdue one day while flying solo, but appeared later that evening carrying his bundled up parachute under his arm. His story was that he had been doing some aerobatics, when, coming round in a slow roll, he found he could not centralize the stick. The ailerons had jammed and the aeroplane continued to roll. He used both hands and as much force as he could apply on the control column but with very little effect. The elevators and rudder were free and he contrived to keep the nose up on the horizon somehow, but the Tiger was otherwise uncontrollable. It was quite impossible to think of landing and so he made sure he was over open country and baled out.

A few people in the mess recalled him saying how much he wanted to experience a parachute jump and found his story about the ailerons jamming very suspect. He was a very ingenuous young man and would go pink in the face denying the charge. Inspection of the wreck, however, showed how the aileron cable had slipped off its pulley and was buried deeply in the wood block beneath it from the force he had obviously applied trying to correct the roll.

The reason why the cable had jumped off the pulley was not established but I had a theory. It could only have happened if slack had suddenly occurred in the cable and I recalled my own experience after I had flick-rolled a Tiger a few times during a flying practice. The flick-roll in the Tiger was strictly verboten as the plane was simply not strong enough to withstand the 'g' forces induced in such a violent manoeuvre. Nevertheless most instructors tried it at some time and no one ever broke a plane in the process, as far as we knew. After my efforts at flick-rolling however, the rigger told me the next day that I could not take my aeroplane out as he was having to re-rig completely the main planes.

"I've only ever seen such distortion once before and that was after the CFI had been flick-rolling! Please don't do it again, Sarge. Too much fucking aggro' in the hangar!"

I had a dodgy moment one night during night flying practice. It was a very dark one and flying was restricted to the circuit. The air raid drill for night flying required the immediate extinction of the flare path for obvious reasons but the alert normally came through in time to get all the aircraft down before turning the lights off. On this particular night however, a Junkers 88 intruder was not detected until the last moment and I was airborne with a pupil in the back seat when the flare path and lead-in lights all went out. I guessed what had happened and flew off to the north to circle the crescent shaped lake at Thornton only a few miles from the circuit. Although I had switched off my navigation lights I was still very aware of the two foot long flame stabbing from the exhaust and I throttled back intending to get as low as possible. It probably saved our lives because at that moment a black shape whooshed past, nearly turning the Tiger on to its back with the violence of its slipstream. The intruder presumably had misjudged the speed of the Tiger, perhaps assuming it to be an operational aircraft, and had overshot badly. I winged the Tiger over into a half-roll and dived back away from the lake. Ten minutes later the Chance Light and the Flare path came on and we were able to land.

It was about this time that the government announced a scheme to be introduced on demobilization for ex-service personnel. Grants were to be made available for various business and professional courses, among which was included architecture. It seemed like a golden opportunity to me, if only such a grant would be sufficient and if only I could qualify for one. I suddenly thought how my attitude had changed since the early days. Now, here I was thinking seriously about after the war.

It was also at this time that my Crown came through, that is the Crown over the Sergeant's stripes denoting the rank of Flight Sergeant - with pay commensurate! It was a funny old life and I was learning fast about it. The Flight Sergeant at ITW had been quite God-like and even the Corporals and Sergeants there had been in awe of him. Now, as a Flight Sergeant myself I had all the intangible extra status that came with it. There was only the Mess President, a Warrant Officer, who was now my senior in the mess. It all meant very little in reality of course, where aircrew rank had not the same significance as it had in other branches of the Service. A Flight Sergeant in the RAF Regiment, say, would have considerable authority over other NCOs and be responsible for a large section of airmen. For me though, the important thing was the extra pay and the evidence that I was no longer a 'sprog' Instructor.

I did have an occasion to pull rank, I suppose, during some night time manoeuvres the RAF Regiment thought up. The idea was to see how the aerodrome could be defended in the event of an enemy landing - the enemy in this case being played by the local Home Guard. The Regiment was in its element, of course, with gun posts manned and men deployed strategically all around the field. The CO had his headquarters in a bunker near the eastern perimeter and 'B' Flight was deployed as the headquarters defence. It was 0200 hours, the low point in a very dark and very cold damp night, when I heard marching feet and shouted orders outside the bunker. It went on for some time, the feet marching to and fro and the shouted commands. I went out and found a fairly newly-arrived Sergeant Freestone drilling the Flight of pupils up and down the road. It seemed an utterly pointless activity and I asked Freestone to stand the Flight at ease and took him to one side. "What the hell are you doing with them?" The Sergeant looked vaguely surprised.

"Keeping them occupied. What do you think? They look bloody untidy just sitting around." I could hardly credit what I was hearing.

"For God's sake, stand them down and go and have a smoke or something." Freestone came up to attention, derisively. "Yes Flight, as you say Flight," and he turned back to dismiss the men.

RAF Desford, 1943

It was customary to have a drag in between trips sitting out on the terrace in front of the crew room. There were usually two or three other instructors there ready for a chat. On this day I was sitting on the terrace having a cigarette when Flight Lieutenant Brookes came out and squatted down next to me. "Congratulations on your Crown, Berry. Not before time, of course."

We sat watching the activity out on the field, occasionally grunting at the more extravagant attempts at landing, or hissing at the sight of some tortured Tiger hanging on its prop twenty feet above the grass. "Would you take a commission, Berry, if it were offered?"

I think I sat up very surprised. "Yes, I would." "I can't think why you haven't been commissioned already." I couldn't think of anything to say to that. "Ah well, if you are keen I'll put your name forward. I'll speak to the CO about it." He slapped the arm of his seat, stood up, nodded amiably and wandered off.

"Well, I'll be buggered..." I looked down at the new, brightly polished Crown over my stripes. "I'll be buggered!"

132

The name of Flight Lieutenant Brookes came up one day many years after the war. I saw a picture of him in uniform in a magazine, which referred to his death in a flying accident some time after the war had ended. Reference was made to his wife who survived him. I wrote to the magazine asking them to forward my letter to Mrs Brookes in which I introduced myself as an old colleague of her husband. Her daughter replied, as her mother was very ill, asking me for as much information about her father as I could remember. She was a very young baby when her father was killed and she hungered for as much detail about him as I could muster. We corresponded a few times thereafter and she finally suggested she flew down to Redhill airport in her Cessna to meet me. Unfortunately, this never happened.

CHAPTER 17

1944

News of my commission came through surprisingly quickly. Within a month of my conversation with Flight Lieutenant Brookes, I was notified by the Air Ministry that I would be duly Gazetted and that meanwhile I should get measured for my uniform. They sent me a voucher to cover the cost for the complete kit which included the uniform, a great coat, Forage and Dress caps, shoes, shirts and socks. I retained my original Battle Dress which was modified only by the changes to the rank insignias. I got a tremendous kick out of going down to Gieves, I think it was, in Piccadilly to be measured and Joan and I celebrated that evening by taking in a film - Noel Coward's 'In Which We Serve'.

When he heard of my commissioning the landlord of the Red Cow produced a magnificent, gilt-braided, three-dimensional cap badge to replace the war-time plastic version I would normally have got from Gieves - a relic from less utilitarian days of peace.

We were home on leave when my commission actually came through. A telegram arrived for 'Pilot Officer' Berry telling me that - "With effect from 1st February 1944, etc...."

I caught the train up to London the next afternoon and put my Pilot Officer's uniform on for the first time feeling incredible conspicuous and self-conscious as I walked back down Piccadilly. I caught the train from Victoria and had to change at Newington for Sittingbourne. My connection was not due for another forty minutes and as I waited on the dark and deserted platform so the air raid siren wailed mournfully. Standing there in the blackness I was then treated to a spectacular display of fireworks. Jerry, in continuous procession, was beating up to London just inshore from the estuary. The guns dispersed all along the corridor followed each plane banging away and speckling the dome of the night with their deadly dots of flak.

"What a funny old welcome," I thought, "but appropriate." I felt too pleased with myself though to feel worried about the air raid even when I heard shrapnel pinging on the platform nearby.

Joan's sister Joyce, who was a couple of years older than Joan, was expecting her first baby in March, a great event for the Wyver family although it would not be the first grandchild. Her eldest sister, Jessie, had already produced and young Anne was a very bright three-year old. Joyce lived a few miles up the road from Sittingbourne, in Gillingham, the least salubrious of the three Medway towns. It had been agreed that Joan would come down to stay for a couple of weeks over the confinement and I got a couple of days leave to bring her down as soon as the baby arrived.

I was driving back to Leicester, through Bedford, when I saw a strikingly attractive girl with long blond hair on a bicycle waiting to turn out from a side road in front of me. I recognised her instantly. It was Marie Roche.

I jammed on the brakes and yanked the car into the side of the road hitting the curb with a thump of rubber. I ejected out over the running board, waving and shouting. "Marie ... Marie Roche."

The girl wobbled her bicycle up to the pavement, alarmed, peering hard. And then she recognised me. "Dennis?"

We said nothing, it seemed like for ages, just grinning at each other widely. It all seemed so amazing. For me she was just the same girl as if the five years had never happened, fresh, faintly freckled and with those fun-lidded blue eyes. "God, it's amazing. You haven't changed a bit. How are you?"

She laughed happily. "Dennis, for heaven's sake, where have you come from?"

"I'm just going back off leave. But what are you doing here, in Bedford?"

"We live here now." She laughed again happily and got off her bicycle, turning towards me.

"Look. Can we have coffee somewhere, or something? There's so much to talk about."

Marie nodded thoughtfully. "There won't be anywhere open now at this time. But why not come back home, there's only mother and me."

"Marvellous. I'll follow you, but don't ride too fast otherwise I'll never keep up. Is it far?" Marie shook her head. "It's just round the corner really. We've only just moved in, so be prepared for the chaos."

As I followed her I wondered what sort of reception I would get from her mother. I always thought she must have known about me way back and yet there was never any sign of it. And what about her father? Where was he? He was a conjurer, or as Marie called him, a prestidigitator. He always looked such a ponderous and miserable man, least of all like an entertainer.

We arrived at an Edwardian terraced house just behind the main road, and leaning her bicycle against the dividing privet hedge Marie let me in through the stained glass front door. Mrs Roche was on her hands and knees on the floor of the kitchen, struggling with a roll of new lino and she seemed to be completely unfazed by my arrival. It was just as if she expected me. There was no explanation of who I was and none asked for, simply, "Look who I met in the High Street mother, Dennis Berry!"

"Hullo Dennis. You really must excuse the muddle, but we only moved in yesterday." It was all so friendly and normal. Within half an hour I had my tunic off and was on my hands and knees cutting and fitting lino alongside the other two.

Mr Roche had died apparently a couple of years earlier and Marie's brother Leslie was away in the army, so it was literally only Marie and her mother. Marie was working in a hairdressing salon doing manicures and presumably learning the trade.

"When do you have to be back on duty?"

"Well, officially I don't have to report for flying until 0900 hours - 9 o'clock that is - tomorrow morning."

"Good. That means you can stay overnight and get off early tomorrow then."

I raised my eyebrows looking at Mrs Roche. The proposal from Marie came as such a surprise - but the whole evening had been one enormous surprise. I felt the same old kick being with her, wanting to put my arm around her, but scared in case she scolded me if I had tried. It never occurred to me to tell her that I was now married. I had slipped back in time, into another life, one I guess I had never properly given up anyway. Mrs Roche thought it a good idea for me to stay too.

"He can sleep in your bed dear, and we can make up the spare for you."

It turned out to be a very busy evening for the three of us, unpacking cases, shifting furniture and for me, laying lino. The activity was punctuated every so often with sandwiches and tea which Marie produced. It was really quite bizarre, an utterly domesticated situation which Marie and her mother seemed to take completely for granted.

Mrs Roche finally suggested that as I would need to get off so early the next morning perhaps bed was in order. Marie took me up to her bedroom which was already very tidy and organized. It was a very feminine room, pink curtains and bedspread, lace mats on the dressing table and everywhere a faint hint of perfume. I undressed self-consciously, peering closely at all the ornaments and paraphernalia about the room. It was like peeping at secrets I had no right to see and yet wanted to look at so much.

I felt a tingle of excitement as I slid down in between the cold sheets of her bed and I lay there in the darkness for a long while thinking about her. We had not had a moment alone during the entire evening and had not even touched hands, but the chemistry was intense. The recollection of how she had failed to turn up that Christmas came back to me. I had never understood what had happened to us.

Then, for the first time, I thought of Joan. But this was unfinished business - actually long before Joan. It was really like laying a ghost. The thought made me laugh out loud and I had to convert the sudden noise into a cough. "Some ghost!" I thought.

"Come on sleepy head. It's seven o'clock."

I woke from a deep sleep. Marie stood smiling down at me holding a cup of tea. She looked marvellously fresh, dressed and with her hair shining golden in the sun streaming through the window behind her. I was very conscious of my own sleepy staleness as I propped myself up on one elbow. She gave me the tea and then backed away from the bedside quickly as if she was a bit confused. She turned away and left the room abruptly and before I even had time to thank her.

Lying in bed that night I had worked out a strategy for seeing her again and before leaving to drive back to Leicester I put my idea. "There's an airfield about three miles north of Bedford called Twinwood Farm. It's not operational. The Yanks use it as an emergency field I believe, but I could fly down one afternoon, probably a Wednesday and perhaps we could meet? What do you think?"

"That would be terrific. I know where you mean. I have Wednesday afternoons off and I could easily cycle out there."

I gave her the camp address at Desford and said I would write and fix a date. We stood facing each other by the car for a long moment. "Marie, it has been wonderful seeing you again." She nodded, not smiling this time.

"Please let's keep our date." I put my hands on her waist and we kissed.

I wrote to her shortly after I got back and suggested I flew down the following week. I got her reply by return post, a long bubbly letter full of her excitement at the prospect of meeting again so soon. My conscience was troubling me enormously now though, and it was probably because of this and the anguish I started feeling that I began viewing my self-indulgence as an act of revenge for what she had done to me five years ago. In this light I could almost excuse myself for what I might be doing to Joan. "I'll take it just so far without hurting Joan, to close that episode for all time."

I flew down immediately after lunch to Twinwood Farm and confirmed that it was a deserted airfield. I saw Marie from the down wind circuit, or at any rate a cyclist I assumed was she, on the perimeter road by the blister hangars. It was her and she waved furiously at me as I taxied over to the hangar apron. I found some chocks, secured the plane, fixed the cockpit covers and put my parachute in the locker behind the rear cockpit in exchange for my forage cap. Then I loped over the grass to meet her. We kissed and hugged and laughed.

"Where the devil are we going - what are we going to do?" and I waved my arm to take in the surrounding countryside.

"Oh, don't worry. We can find somewhere nice to sit and talk. There's heaps to talk about, isn't there? How long have we got?"

I put my arm round her waist and took her bicycle from her. "We've got until about half five, so let's hide this thing and then find somewhere to sit." It was obviously more important to hide and protect her bicycle than my aeroplane. We put it inside a brick shelter next to the blister hangar and in the process Marie found a rusty iron ladder leading up to the roof of the shelter. She immediately started climbing it in spite of my protests. "For heaven's sake Marie, you're not a schoolgirl anymore."

She stopped at the top of the ladder, grinning down at me. "Come on Dennis. Where's your sense of adventure?" I was keeping well back from the foot of the ladder carefully not looking up as the breeze billowed her skirt.

"Please Dennis, come on," she insisted and I was finally compelled to join her on the ladder while she paused at the top waiting for me. The view from the top of the shed, however, was disappointing and so we climbed down again with Marie insisting that I should go first.

We had caught a glimpse of a river, probably the Ouse, while we were up there and we decided that we should walk in that direction. The meadowland at the side of the river was indeed very attractive and we selected a soft grassy bank on which to sit. Marie was wearing a high-necked dark blue dress with a polka dot pattern.

"Your dress sets off your complexion beautifully. I don't think I've ever seen you in anything but pastel colours before."

"I didn't know what to wear. Whether to dress down for the country, or to dress up for you." We both laughed and then became solemn as we looked into each other's eyes. She swayed towards me and our lips met and we kissed.

We laid there making love for hours, indifferent to the world and while our lips melded and our tongues intimately fenced I explored the contours of her body, frustrated by the absence of buttons and openings in her dress. For me it was a rediscovery of everything I thought I had lost.

My thoughts were utterly confused. In my heart I knew I was deeply in love with her still but I daren't admit it. The thought was an awful betrayal of Joan. But I wanted her like mad. If only I were free ... if only I had waited just as she had ...

I saw her again the following Wednesday when I motored down to pick up Joan. It was a weird, even surreal, afternoon in retrospect. Marie said a Fair had arrived and could we go and see it? We toured the stalls and the sideshows, failed to win anything, but enjoyed the cacophony, the screams and the thumping tempo of the music everywhere. Then we came to the big carousel with its prancing horses, the bright brass and the lights reflecting as if in a kaleidoscope, and the whoomp - humpf - humpf of its organ. The noise was overwhelming. Marie had to go on it and we climbed on to a great golden horse, me in front and Marie behind. The thing started winding up faster and faster, the horses riding up and down their brass poles, the encircling faces streaming into blurs of white and the blaring, thumping organ blasting out its sound in physical energy. The centrifugal force built up with the rotational speed and where I would have been comfortable holding just myself, with Marie clinging around my waist I was having to support both of us. It became as much as I could do to hang on. My knuckles were white as I gripped the brass pole and my thighs began to ache as I clenched them harder and harder around the wooden flanks of the bucking horse. And still the speed increased and with it the giddy sideways force. I began to think I wouldn't be able to hang on much longer and that we would both be flying off into the crowd. But it went faster still becoming an absolute nightmare. Sweat was blurring my vision. I could hear Marie screaming behind me, her arms tugging to pull me off my seat.

Then, just at the point of catastrophe, the strain began to lessen and the speed of the roundabout slowed. My vision cleared and I felt I could breath normally once more.

We walked down to the river after that and sat in the long grass and made love until it was time for me to leave.

Now, as an old man, as I write this I wonder at my self-indulgence, the betrayal of my wife. God knows she loved me and was true in her loyalty and faithfulness. I can remember, however, the enormous temptation it was. I had never got over my affair with Marie and here it was revived in all of its overwhelming intensity. In my self-indulgence I obviously had no thought either, or very little thought, of what I might be doing to Marie. I do recall, in my confusion, that I reasoned I was getting some sort of revenge, and then again, if I thought about it at all, I was really only concluding some unfinished business from my youth. Either way, I can see no justification now for my behaviour at that time and there is no way I can excuse it. I can only hope to expunge my guilt by the telling.

CHAPTER 18

As the spring advanced in 1944 so the air war in Europe heated up to even greater fury. Rumours that we were preparing for the big day, the invasion, were hot news in the mess. The US Airforce by day and the RAF by night were pounding the enemy's rear areas across the channel, the marshalling yards and the airfields, which would be key in any invasion plan. All coastal areas bordering the channel were now banned to tourists and the UK was beginning to look like one vast armed camp. On the 10th April 3,600 tons of bombs were dropped in a single raid on Germany, the heaviest raid so far of the war. But even this was soon exceeded when 4,500 tons were dropped by way of celebrating Hitler's birthday.

I was still flying quite hard, although not so intensively as in the previous summer. This was perhaps unfortunate as it gave me too much time to think. I was utterly confused as to what I could, and should, do about Marie. She was writing to me regularly, cheerful, chatty letters, which were always signed off with her love and affection. I knew I should write and tell her that I was married and that I was not only betraying Joan in the process, but that I was also behaving appallingly to Marie as well. But to have found her like this was so wonderful, I simply could not face up to losing her again. I felt utterly desolate, just as if every one else was going to the party except me. It was like my childhood all over again. I was reminded of that awful feeling of desolation I would have on a Sunday afternoon when my brother and two sisters would go out leaving me alone with my parents. They would say I was too young to go with them, and Dad was too old to understand and to offer me any comfort. Strangely, and in my blackest moods, I found comfort being with Joan.

I felt particularly gloomy the Wednesday immediately after Joan came back. The wind was far too strong to do any meaningful instruction although the sky was clear and with brilliant sunshine. I took my aeroplane up for some solo flying and as I climbed up away from the circuit I had the sudden notion of seeing how high I could get the

Tiger to fly. Its official ceiling was said to be about 13,500 feet although I had never heard of anyone getting anywhere near this figure. The Tiger was not equipped with oxygen so I knew I would not be able to get much above 10,000 feet anyway.

It took me twelve minutes or so to get up to 5,000 feet, the normal height for teaching aerobatics, and another few minutes to reach 6,000 feet, as high as one normally went to teach the procedure for restarting the engine in flight. After this it was unfamiliar territory, but I carried on climbing. After another fifteen or so minutes of flying I saw the altimeter touch 9,000 feet. It was bitterly cold with only my flying jacket on and without my leggings and I began to think it was a daft idea anyway, but I carried on holding the nose up.

At 9,500 feet, with the horizon now sharply delineated and everything below it lost in a darkening blue haze, I decided to give up. It was so cold, I had little idea where I was and it would take me another thirty minutes or so to regain the circuit anyway. So I throttled back and started gliding into the mist below, but giving a short burst of throttle every few minutes to prevent a possible engine cut-out in the extreme cold. Everything was fine until suddenly, at about 8,000 feet, I had a blinding pain behind my eyes. I could see nothing, the tears were streaming down from my goggles and the pain was screwing the top of my head off. I opened the throttle instinctively and levelled the aeroplane onto the horizon, more to give myself time to think than anything else. I knew what the problem was - either my Eustachian tubes, or my sinus cavities, were blocked. I tried the obvious remedy of holding my nose and swallowing, but nothing I could do seemed to have the slightest effect. Every time I tried to lose height so the excruciating pain returned. "This is crazy," I thought, "I can't stay up here for ever."

I looked up at the petrol gauge on the tank in the middle of the top wings. It registered less than a quarter of a tank, or under half an hour of flying, not very reassuring if I had to spend much time in trying to lose height.

I tried once more and got down to just under 7,000 feet before the pain stopped me again. "I can't even bale out." The thought of the pain intensifying as I came down beneath my brolly was too awful to contemplate. "I'll bloody well have to though, as soon as the petrol gives out. I couldn't fly this bloody thing in like this."

I tried with fresh urgency to reduce height and this time got down to 6,300 feet before the pain forced me to open up the engine. I reckoned I had about twenty minutes flying left. "As long as I come out near the 'drome I should be OK," this more in hope than conviction.

In fact the last few thousand feet were easier and the closer I got to earth the lesser became the pain. I was very close to the airfield by now and I finally glided in with about five minutes of fuel to spare.

I found that everyone had already left the dispersal as flying had long since been washed out except, that is, for the Flight Commander and the Timekeeper. She was particularly upset. "The opportunity for an early finish and you have to go overdue!" The flight commander was equally petulant, if briefer. "Where the hell have you been?"

I gave him some plausible story about endurance testing, coupled with apologies and calmed the man down. I made no reference to my experiences as I tried to lose height from 9,000 feet. One didn't draw attention to medical conditions like that in a hurry and without first thinking about it very carefully!

CHAPTER 19

On the 14th April my posting on to operations came through.

It was a shock, although not totally unexpected. If the invasion was due this summer the war could well be over within a year making it logical to start winding down the flying training programme and releasing many of the instructors involved. A few from the mess had already been posted, like George Inman who had gone on to fly Dakotas, the American DC.3, a lumbering twin-engined work horse. A very worried-looking George had flown in recently, just before his posting out to Burma, not at all happy about the prospects of flying over 'all that jungle.' Someone else had flown back in a very purposeful looking Hurricane, the first I had inspected closely. It looked enormous next to a Tiger Moth, with its four 20mm Hispano guns jutting from the leading edges of its wings, a menacing great dark bird.

Another instructor was said to have been posted to fly an army glider as part of the invasion force. Having landed behind the enemy's lines he was supposed then to make his own way back to pick up another glider full of troops for a further trip. This was said to have been 'duff gen' - someone's idea of a sick joke - but, nasty thought, someone was going to have to fly them!

My posting in some ways was a relief. At least I was going on to single engined fighters and assumed that I would stay in England, for a time anyway. I was to report to No 5 (P) AFU – Pilot Advanced Flying Unit - at Ternhill where initially I would be flying Miles Masters.

Joan was very upset but did her best to conceal her feelings, giving me as much support as she could. Our comfortable life style obviously was about to be completely shattered, although it was agreed that Joan would stay on at Park Drive meanwhile until my ultimate posting was known. I greeted the news with confused emotions, not least of which was misery at the disruption of what I now realised had become a very agreeable existence in Desford. At the same time there was a fearful thrill at the prospect of at last flying something worthwhile. I had spent nearly 1,500 hours on Tiger Moths and similar aircraft and it was time for a change. I doubted if I would ever achieve my first ambition though to fly the Spitfire because aerial combat was changing at this stage of the war away from fighter sweeps and close bomber support to army support with ground strafing aircraft capable of taking out tanks, trains and anything that moved - and bore a swastika. Everyone in fact was now talking about the Typhoon and the Tempest. Whether I would ever be able to fly such things however, after so much Tiger bashing was a thought which lurked uncomfortably somewhere.

The other emotion I felt concerned my dilemma over Marie. The posting in this sense was extremely timely in that I felt absolved from taking any immediate action. So I wrote and told her about the posting and promised to send her my new address when I had it. I reasoned that this would give me time to think it all out. My conscience remained deeply troubled though, particularly at the anguish I felt at leaving Joan. Those last few days were extremely miserable for both of us, particularly the last night before I was due to leave. It was the worst one of my life and I lay awake in the cool night air dreading the dawn as it approached and dreading the goodbyes it would bring.

I arrived in my Morris 10/4 at Ternhill on the 24th April 1944. It was obviously a peacetime RAF station of some impressive scale, from the horizon-dominating hangars to the red brick multi-storied WAAF barrack blocks. The course pilots were not housed very splendidly however, but were in two-storey prefabricated hutments, four of them to a room. The mess, in contrast, was extremely comfortable and the other pilots on the course, mostly from Canada, were very agreeable. I chummed up immediately with a Flight Lieutenant Alan Bloom, a laid-back English public school type who seemed to take everything just as it came.

My first flight was within a couple of days, a so-called navigational exercise in a twin-engined Anson. The experience of flying in this staid, lumbering old trainer, which so many bomber pilots had flown at Service Flying Training School before going on to Wellingtons, Lancasters, or whatever, was memorable even if the exercise itself was completely redundant other than for the Canadians. The likes of me had already spent hundreds, if not thousands of hours teaching pilot navigation in this country and hardly needed this fifty minute trip.

"Just like the mob. Do everything by the book and make sure that nobody thinks." In response, Alan half-raised an eyebrow. It really was not worth a comment. I had foolishly sat by the pilot and thereby earned the privilege of winding up the non-hydraulic undercarriage.

"Not a good beginning," Alan said, looking around and then nodding down at my exertions with the undercart wheel.

My next trip was in a Master 11, when I met up with my instructor, Flight Sergeant Gurney, a bored and uncommunicative individual. I could never make up my mind as to whether Gurney was actually bored with his role or whether his reserve arose from a fear of the aeroplane. He was certainly full of the Master's failings, like "Watch your airspeed and don't stall on take off, otherwise you've had it ... She spins like a bitch." "If you get engine failure on take off you've had it anyway." "You see the twin exhausts under the stub wings, well, the petrol tanks are above those! Remember that if you ever have to make a belly landing" and so on!

The office seemed to be vast after the Tiger, big enough in which to swing the proverbial cat. Although only a foot higher than the Tiger and with a foot wider wing span the Master felt enormous in comparison. The cockpit drill and vital actions assumed major importance, with the inclusion of items such as pitch control - "Try taking off in coarse pitch and you won't." Radiator gills - "You won't taxi far with them closed, you'll just cook everything." Switch on the IFF (Identification Friend or Foe) - "If you don't the Ack Ack boys will use you for target practice." Flaps up - "If you taxi with them down the riggers will have your balls for breakfast - Sir." There followed detailed explanations of the fuel, ignition, lighting, coolant, hydraulic and braking systems before we taxied out for the first flight.

The engine was started from a 'trolley-ack', which comprised massive accumulators wheeled around on the tarmac and plugged in to the Bristol Mercury XX nine-cylinder radial air-cooled engines. I became only too aware of the 870 hp in front of me as the prop kicked over and the engine spluttered into life with an horrendous clatter of noise. Running up with the hood closed was essential although the noise was still overpowering, causing the entire airframe to vibrate furiously.

The Master was a heavy-looking aeroplane, with its large radial engine, massive three-bladed prop and large glass canopy over the tandem seats. At least that was how it struck me. Its wing formation was reminiscent of the Junkers 87 with the wing roots sloping down from the fuselage and the outer sections set at a slight dihedral angle. The wheels retracted and rotated in the process up into the wing roots.

Having asked for and received permission to take off, Gurney swung out onto the runway and rammed the throttle up to its stop. The take off surprised me. Apart from the enormous acceleration there was little familiar 'getting the tail up' for flying speed and we seemed to take off at a similar angle as we taxied. The prop clearance on the runway was probably too critical for much else.

We climbed steeply up to about 3,000 feet and Gurney told me to take over. My first impression was less of flying an aeroplane but more of flying an engine. There was so much power out there in front, nearly seven times greater than anything I had ever flown before, that I was reminded of the current cartoon of P/O Prune - 'Going round on one engine,' wherein he straddles a fat aeroplane-less engine. The controls, although all hydraulic, felt relatively heavy, but the aeroplane trimmed beautifully thanks to the tail and rudder trimmers. With a cruising speed of 230 mph at 5,000 feet and a top straight and level speed of 260 mph, the aeroplane was certainly no slouch.

The next few trips covered all the dramatic safety drills, like spinning, abandoning the aircraft and action in the event of fire, none of which really registered on me as they were designed to do. I was still fighting to come to terms with simply flying this aeroplane and trying to land it with conviction. The landing in fact was not too difficult once you screwed your bottle up enough. You simply flew it in with engine and flaps and gauged your rate of descent with the throttle. It was easier than the Tiger in fact, much easier. But I didn't feel very confident. I was always haunted by the spectre of engine failure on take-off. "Why the hell did Gurney make such an issue of it? If he'd never mentioned it I wouldn't have thought of it."

Then on night flying one night someone did have an engine cut out on take off and he augured straight in. The buzz went round - "The bloody things aren't safe." But the flying went on and I got down to the serious business of flying a Master.

It was not just another aeroplane, it was another era completely, like jumping from Stephenson's Rocket on to the Flying Scotsman, or from a sailing dinghy into Campbell's Blue Bird. Everyone had to make this transition, I knew, but for someone who had spent not just fifty hours, but one thousand five hundred hours, driving the Flying Scot was more than just a bit different. The Master was quite a manoeuvrable plane in fact, once one forgot the comparison, and you could pull a lot of 'G' in steep turns, although that was another way of spinning in if you pulled it too tight. It was the mental adjustment I had to make constantly, from jiggling a box kite on the breezes to sitting behind that raging motor up front which dragged me along regardless. The entire process of flying this engine was deciding in which direction you wanted to point it - and then following - if a bit breathlessly. After the Tiger I really couldn't see a great deal of finesse in the process. Perhaps as time went on I would learn.

I did just over three hours dual before I was checked out and sent off on my first solo. Although nothing would ever come up to that first solo of all in the Tiger Moth this was quite an event. The enormous kick in the back as I opened the throttle and the sensation of sitting astride so much power as I climbed away was uniquely thrilling. My heart was racing and I was sitting mentally on the edge of my seat, feet spread and flexing on the rudder bar, right hand around the spade grip of the control column and my left hand pushing the rimmed knob of the throttle up to its stop. All went well as I cruised around the circuit, turned across wind and then powered the plane down onto the runway with the now familiar screech of tyres on concrete.

Thereafter there was a great deal to absorb, like RT procedures, gunnery, instrument flying and night flying. It was quite novel to head off above the clouds somewhere and to beat up some looming cumulus peaks without having to worry about where the hell you might finish up. An appeal over the RT for a QDR - a compass reciprocal course to fly for base - a brief transmission to give them a fix - and there you were - home. Not that I once had to request a QDR because I was actually lost! But it was fun hearing the WAAF's chirruping away in the ether.

Flight Sergeant Gurney never did demonstrate spin recovery to me in the Master, simply because he never allowed the spin to develop fully in the first place. No sooner had the wing flicked over at the point of stall so he banged on opposite lock and pulled the nose up again. Not that I was overly disappointed at the time.

The most tedious and boring activity, however, was simulated night flying. The runways were equipped with sodium flares and the instruments in the cockpit were all similarly illuminated with sodium bulbs. The pupil due to undergo this torture was obliged to don glasses which were opaque to everything except sodium light, and thus equipped he entered a world of bible black through which he could only see his instruments and the flare path. So on the brightest of sunny days he was doomed to fly his aeroplane in stygian night, relieved only by the glimmerings of the flare path and the glow of his instrument panel. The tedium of throttling on to that orange perspective of lights, thrusting the throttle through its gate, holding the nose in between the diminishing vee and then climbing up on the artificial horizon, up to circuit height, round for an approach and landing, and so on, was bad enough for the pupil but screamingly tedious for the instructor. The pattern would only be broken when we flew away from the circuit to do a cross country on instruments.

It was certainly spectacular country over which to fly, with some dramatic mountainous landscape only ten to fifteen minutes away westwards and the Rivers Mersey and Dee to the north where the grey/black conurbation of Liverpool squeezes the Mersey tight shut. I enjoyed the flying when I was not having to work at it too much which, however, was most of the time.

The buzz in the mess was all about the impending invasion. It was going to happen any time now, for sure. The build-up, both physically and psychologically, was too intense to be anything but for the real thing. The blasting of the rear areas both day and night was intensifying and Mustangs, Lightnings and Thunderbolts were working the daylight shifts around the clock, hammering the enemy wherever he could be found.

Then on the 6th June the news burst - the RAF and the US 8th Airforce had been pounding the coastal batteries over the Channel since dawn and several thousand ships had been converging on landings soon after 5.00 am. It was D-Day and we were going back into Europe! The news probably gave a fresh bite to the flying with everyone moaning that it could all be over before we had a chance to get involved.

"There's little hope of that I guess. It's a long way to Berlin and after that we'll all be shipped out to Burma!" Alan Bloom's words were too prophetic to be amusing. I, for one, had been hoping for a nice quiet end to the war, flying my sorties out from Manston, or Biggin Hill perhaps, but certainly nothing as hazardous as chasing Japs to Tokyo and flying off grass strips out of the jungle.

Then the following week news came through about a new weapon Hitler had mounted, the V1 flying bomb! It appeared to be a jet propelled pilotless aeroplane which was coming in over the coast at 400 plus miles an hour. Nothing was quick enough to intercept it unless you had height and could dive on it. Many of them were getting through although someone developed a technique of tipping them over with his wing as he formatted on them. They were awesome things to blow up at close range, they said!

The Master was fitted with a camera gun operated by a trigger on the control column and one of the more enjoyable exercises was practicing aerial combat with another pupil. Convinced that I had successfully shot down my enemy, I would subsequently view the evidence in the projection room only to discover that I was either out of range, or that my deflection shooting was too wide. I began to appreciate the difficulty of shooting anything down, let alone 'doodlebugs'.

We also had frequent practice on the clay pigeon range where I improved my marksmanship considerably and this did have a bearing upon aerial 'shooting', although everyone made the same mistake initially of 'opening fire' too early and way out of range. Tucking right up behind the other plane, far closer than instinct suggested and then tugging the Master in tightly for the deflection shot and I began to get better results. It was getting in close enough which did the trick and then pulling enough G to stay on his tail. I was convinced I had shot down at least half a dozen of my fellow course pupils, although they all assured me of my own demise - too often for any complacency!

"You've got to fly it roughly - to hell with skid or slip. Pull the bugger round - and you might stay alive!" One had to fly it roughly, I knew this well enough by now, but finesse and precision had been the goal in flying for so long, it came very hard to fly badly!

In mid-June we had a week of night flying which comprised interminable circuits and bumps, varied only with the mandatory over-shoots wherein one rammed the throttle open at the point of touch down, retracted the wheels and the flaps, retrimmed and climbed away for another circuit. It was a great relief from the tedium of the circuits to fly away from the aerodrome on a cross country, or even to go beacon flying. It was a strange other-world experience, flying at night, particularly when it was moonless. One felt as if suspended motionless in a black and albeit noisy place. Within the cockpit there was the faint glow from the instruments, just enough to see them by, but outside the canopy was nothing, no movement, no lights anywhere except for the flare path and away from that no reference points whatsoever. The blind flying instruments told you whether you were flying level, banking, climbing, or descending, but one had no sensations about the aeroplane's attitude and you had to place total faith in those dancing needles in the blind flying panel. Apart from the otherwise reassuring engine noise, it would have been extremely peaceful. The thermal currents, which at day disturbed the plane and called for constant control adjustments, were quiescent at night, adding to the motionless illusion. I enjoyed the sense of being unplugged from the world, the unreality of the moment. The nearest I had ever got to the sensation before, and that was a million years away, was driving alone at night in the country.

It was about a month later, back on day flying, that I had a reoccurrence of my sinus pain. I was on a gunnery exercise with my instructor and was losing height from 14,000 feet to return to base when I had the blinding pain behind my eyes. My instructor was quite shaken and radioed base to ask for advice. It took only a few minutes before they were able to tell him to lose height very gradually, no doubt having telephoned the duty Medical Officer. As before, when I was flying alone, we edged down slowly to allow me to acclimatise gradually to the increased pressure and we finally landed a half hour or so later.

The MO saw me in the Sick Bay and told me that my sinus cavities were probably blocked and that he would send me over to the RAF Hospital at Cosford for treatment. Meanwhile I would be admitted into the Sick Bay and to go back and collect my pyjamas and toothbrush!

So began an amazing week of Whitehall-like farce! I was admitted into the station hospital, into a ward which contained four beds with an adjoining ablutions. I felt perfectly fit and yet the regime required me to don pyjamas and to go to bed. The other three beds were occupied by Canadian Course Pilots, none of whom I had previously met but all of whom seemed as fit as I was.

There were four nurses who shared the day and night shifts, all of them extremely attractive and all devoted to making the life of their patients as happy as possible. Indeed it sometimes seemed as if we four patients were there solely for the benefit of the nurses so that they could practice and develop their bedside manners! Four lusty men, all in near prime health, locked away with four attractive women, could lead to all sorts of trouble.

After the first few nights I awoke to see one of the WAAF nurses, a well-built young blond, creep into the ward and climb into the bed of one of the Canadians. After lots of grunts and grinding bed springs I saw the nurse disappearing through the door struggling as she went to button up her white uniform.

The following day this particular nurse asked me to go out to the scales in the corridor as she had to record my weight. Before I got on the scales she attempted to guess what it would be, first feeling my biceps and then exploring up and down my thighs. She got it nearly right with much giggling and so I suggested it was my turn.

"I reckon you must be around eight stone," and I started feeling her biceps through her uniform. Her protests were not really meant to stop me as I started groping up her skirt above her knees. She was enjoying it as much as I. How far I might have got though I never found out because someone came into the corridor through the swing door just at that moment - and I was up on my feet like a twanging bowstring.

The next morning I was picked up outside the Sick Bay by a WAAF driver in a small van to be taken to the RAF Hospital at Cosford. There were a couple of airmen in the van and I rode in the front with the driver. She was extremely attractive with a tightly belted tunic which bulged out very satisfactorily over her figure. It seemed as if the Whitehall farce was still running because this girl then started telling me about her sex life. She said she was getting married in a few weeks' time but that meanwhile she was enjoying her weekends in Shrewsbury - usually with a different officer from the mess each time.

"We pick up a cab outside the station and I change into civvies as we drive into Shrewsbury. Then we book into a decent hotel."

"Of course, with an officer you would have to I suppose," I said, as I thought lecherously of this attractive young girl peeling her blouse and skirt off beside me. "Doesn't your future husband object to such things?" "No. Why should he? He was the one who first started it with me when he was stationed here." It obviously seemed quite logical to her.

"So why should I object?" I stared sidelong at her, admiring her pert nose and full lips in profile. She caught me staring and laughed.

"Would you like to spend a weekend with me in Shrewsbury?" I spluttered and then caught up with the conversation again.

"Good God. Yes. Of course I would ... Very much." She laughed again and twinkled her eyes at me. "Great. You're on, but not this weekend coming. I'm already fixed up. Next weekend?"

"Er ... yes, of course."

It fortunately gave me something to think about during the next few miserable hours. The Medical Officer who saw me told me that he was going to drain my sinuses - a simple operation done with a local anaesthetic. Fine!

I waited for an hour alone in a white-walled cubicle, thinking mostly about a weekend in Shrewsbury with a pretty young WAAF whom I was still picturing without her blouse and skirt. Occasionally, though, my thoughts would slip into the present domain wherein I was about to have my sinuses drained - and the bra and pants image would disappear with a jolt!

The MO eventually returned carrying two steel skewers with blobs of cotton wool on their ends. "Head right back. That's it. You won't feel a thing. This will deaden all the pain," and he proceeded to poke the skewers up my nostrils. It was quite true, I didn't feel anything above vague discomfort as the skewers entered my nose.

"We'll leave them there for a few minutes," and the MO disappeared once more leaving me sitting with two steel rods like knitting needles projecting from my face. They crossed each other about seven inches in front of my nose. "That's probably about the right distance to synchronise your guns," I thought.

The MO returned and twanged the ends of the steel rods. "Can you feel anything?"

I had to admit that apart from the musical note generated somewhere within my skull I could not actually feel a thing.

The MO pulled the rods out and then approached me with an altogether more formidable looking contraption. It was a bit like a giant bottle opener with two prongs and a central rod within which was a long screw. I began to get the picture and totally lost all interest in Shrewsbury.

155

What followed was not painful, but was extremely disagreeable. While I did not actually feel the screw thing penetrate anything I certainly heard it crunch through the bone into my sinus cavities. When it was all over I had nothing worse than a minor nosebleed and this had quite stopped by the time I got back to Ternhill.

I was glad that it was a different WAAF who took me back. I could not have coped with a bleeding nose and more sex!

CHAPTER 20

Joan was a very self-contained person with great inner resources and of the two I was probably more upset by our separation than she. Joan tended to view life as a series of trials, each of which had to be confronted and either overcome or, failing this, ignored. She had a way of snorting to dismiss what she saw as unintelligent sentiment, thereby leaving no time in her philosophy for regret. She did miss me obviously but with the encouragement of Mrs Davey, the arch pragmatist around whom it was impossible to mope, she got on with her life with great determination.

She kept up a constant flow of cheerful letters to me, full of the nonconsequential comings and goings at Park Drive and sometimes relaying the news from Kent. I learnt how Prince had caused a bird to die from heart failure by pretending that he was about to chase it, how Micky was making yet another balsa wood glider - since the last one was lodged in the tree at the end of the garden - and how Mrs Davey had made a marvellous carrot cake last weekend and so on.

Mrs Davey had told her she should go out more instead of sitting around the house every evening and so she joined a local keep-fit class. Nelly Benstead, Flight Lieutenant Benstead's wife from Desford, was there and Joan was able to keep up to date with the news from the camp although she rarely passed any of this on to me. Her sister Joyce and the new baby were doing fine and Joan kept writing to say how much she would like to see them again. I wrote back and suggested that she should go down and that she should take a week off from the office to make it worthwhile. Joan was very reluctant, however, as it seemed unfair to do something so pleasurable without me.

News from home included the item that Vie was in Glasgow where Ron had recently been posted. They were staying in digs with a retired doctor and his wife who were making a great fuss of them all and particularly of young Michael. Vie had written saying, "The doctor is a dear, quite old, like Grandpa Viner was when he was about sixty five!"

She was very impressed, Joan said, by Glasgow and the Glaswegians but said everywhere looked so grey and drab.

"The houses are so strongly built all of grey slate stone, much thicker than ours and the women of all classes carry their young children in plaid shawls wrapped right round their bodies and that of the children." She complained too about having to queue up for everything, "even for wool," and about the shortages of some essential foods such as milk and of the non-existence of eggs. I thought wryly of the excellent food I had always had in the RAF, even as an 'erk', particularly the great doorsteps of bread and butter at tea-time which were then spread with thick strawberry jam such as the poor civvies had not seen in years.

Ron was swatting very hard for some exams, Vie said, which were due to be finished in a few more weeks, "then home again.". Presumably Vie would be "home again," but Ron would be back at his post on the Kent coast once more, if he were lucky, and if not over in France somewhere perhaps, Joan wrote.

After the Cosford Hospital excursion I was pronounced fit to fly and I returned once more to the course. I had missed out on quite a bit of flying meanwhile and had a lot of catching up to do. One element of this was converting to the Hawker Hurricane. Some of my colleagues on the course had already taken the Hurricane up and there was an on-going buzz in the mess and at dispersal about their reactions and experiences. Everyone was in love with it, although most comments were made with a trace of awe.

"It's a real beauty to fly, easier than the Master" - seemed to be a consensus opinion.

The transition from the Master to the Hurricane was certainly a simpler step than had been the transition from the Tiger Moth to the Master. We were still flying the Master of course, for dual instruction on instrument flying, formation, low flying, gunnery and the like, but occasionally we were allowed off in the Hurricane for type experience.

The one we were flying was the Mark I I A with the Merlin XX engine of 1,185 bhp giving it about 330 mph at 20,000 feet, 80 mph more than the Master. It was a big aeroplane, bigger than the Master that is, with its 5 feet greater wingspan. It did not feel bigger however, once airborne, and its cockpit was in fact less roomy although one sat quite high in the fuselage and had a very clear view all around particularly forwards over the long sloping nose of the Merlin - that is when airborne but not on the ground taxiing.

Only one basic version of the Hurricane was really ever produced, the Mark I, initially with its Merlin I I or I I I engine and a single stage supercharger. The major change thereafter, as far as performance was concerned, was with the introduction of the more powerful Merlin XX with its two-speed supercharger. This was in the Mark I I version. There were many variants in terms of the armaments however, from eight and twelve Browning machine guns, to four 20mm Hispano cannon and then two 40mm Vickers cannon in conjunction with two .303 Brownings. Other versions included racks for 250 and 500lb bombs and droppable fuel tanks as on the highly successful tactical Hurri-Bomber. The Mark I I A had the original eight Browning machine guns mounted in the wings and with which it had earned its reputation during the Battle of Britain.

I approached my first flight in the fighter with excitement and apprehension, excitement at the prospect of flying a front line machine, the first monoplane fighter at the end of a line of biplanes from the Sopwith Camel to the Gloucester Gladiator, and apprehension from the knowledge that I would be on my own. There could be no dual checkout this time and whatever I found happening as I pushed the throttle open I would have to sort out for myself.

My instructor walked me around the plane for five minutes pointing out various characteristics while I tried my damnedest to concentrate on his every word. Everything was important and I had to remember everything, but the plane had such an enormous presence with its aggressive humpback and widespread undercarriage which gave it a powerful crouching stance ... and I suddenly realized I had not been listening to what the man was saying. "God, I hope it wasn't vital!"

He told me to climb up into the cockpit. With my right foot in the stirrup I got my left foot up on to the wing and then heaved myself into the cockpit. Everything came to hand easily, the familiar blind flying panel with its standard layout in the centre, the rev counter, boost, oil pressure, fuel pressure, fuel contents, oil and radiator temperature gauges to the right and the undercarriage indicator switches, magneto switches, engine starter and oxygen regulator control and gauges on the left. The reflector gunsight was straight ahead above the panel, the throttle control, mixture control and airscrew control levers at the side with the elevator trim and rudder trim neatly to hand.

My instructor spent the next half hour explaining the take off and landing procedures and the general flying characteristics and then after a few cautionary words told me I was fit to go.

I walked back to the dispersal with him to collect my parachute and to sign out. It was a very important moment, one I had been dreaming about since childhood. As I walked back to the Hurricane, dark and looming against the low afternoon sun, I recalled the little model of a Hawker Fury I had made from the kit Ron had given me ... it seemed like yesterday.

A member of the ground crew fussed over me, helping me into the cockpit, passing my Sutton Harness over my shoulders and giving the windscreen a quick wipe over. I ran the Merlin up amidst the familiar fury of noise and vibration, checked the revs, throttled back and as the plane settled down once more on its tyres waved the chocks away.

As I taxied out I suddenly felt very lonely, but the moment passed, there was so much to think about and to do. Forward vision as I taxied was poor, even with the seat raised. The plane felt massively sturdy as it straddled along on its wide undercart. I parked at the entrance to the runway, completed my cockpit check and then instinctively lifted my head to peer quickly around the sky as I had done so many thousands of times before, but this time over the tapering platforms of the Hurricane's wings either side and then up along the massive girth of the long sloping nose of the Merlin.

This was it and thumbing the wireless transmit I asked for permission to take off. The casual voice of control crackled affirmatively in my ears and I gunned the Hurricane on to the runway. If I had had time to think about it I would have confessed to feeling terrified at that moment. The acceleration was enormous. I felt myself pinned back in the seat as the aircraft leapt forwards along the runway, the tail came up and moments later I was airborne. With the airspeed indicator winding up rapidly, I pulled the nose up into the climb and trimmed - more by reflex than reason. The rate of climb was quite astonishing, prompting me to throttle back to climbing revs. It was all happening very quickly, but it felt instinctively right and as time went on this feeling increased.

At 3,000 feet I dropped the nose to the horizon, throttled back and trimmed for cruising. I flew straight and level for a while and consciously tried to relax and to take in what was happening. It was important to check the view of the wings and the bonnet against the horizon and the sky and to become familiar with this new aeroplane I was flying. It was all OK. It handled so easily. It surprised me, this. The plane had looked so heavy and clumsy on the ground, but now it felt precise and responsive and light and not so different from the Master in fact. It was inevitable to make comparisons with the Master, of course, but these were invidious. This aeroplane was a delight and felt a natural. I settled back and gained my second wind, as it were. With increasing confidence I began to weave the plane around, although gently enough at first. I rolled it over into a steep turn, pulling the stick back into my stomach, tightening the turn up until I was pulling quite a lot of 'G'. It felt rock steady and if I could stand the 'G', would obviously go much tighter. Then I tried the feel of the controls at various speeds, first throttling back to reduce the airspeed down as low as I dared, although still above stalling - I wasn't ready for that yet! I was impressed by the amount of control I retained right down to what must have been close to the stall. Then I put the nose down into a fairly steep dive and held it as the airspeed wound up quickly to pass

400. I pulled it up again fiercely, my body pressing down like a ton weight, my arms pinned to my thighs. The horizon dropped away and I held the nose up to the sky, rocketing up, throttle fully open, the Merlin singing away full bore, the airspeed holding. I had never done an upward roll before, never having flown a plane capable of such a manoeuvre, but now I pressed the stick over and watched the horizon wind past the window a full turn before easing the nose over at the top of the loop and rolling out to level flight.

I was at 5,000 feet and the late afternoon horizon was drawn sharply as a slate blue mist line beneath the orange blue sky above. I sat there breathing quickly, my pulse rate competing with the rev counter. I never dreamt I would be pushing it like this on the first flight, which was only supposed to be a few circuits and bumps anyway, but it was a clear indication of how I felt about the aeroplane.

"You'd better see if you can get this thing back on the deck, you silly sod!" and I started reducing height to regain the circuit. The landing in fact was easy. I brought the Hurricane in over the boundary, surprised at the low approach speed, more like a Tiger Moth than the Master, flying it down with the throttle, right down to kiss the runway with a perfect three pointer.

The course was winding up now to its conclusion and speculation was beginning among us as to our next move. It was anticipated that we would be posted for a few weeks to an Operational Training Unit where we would be flying either Hurricanes or Typhoons and learning how to blow up trains and the like, before posting on to a squadron.

The war in Europe was going well, the allies had just opened the second front in France, with landings along the coast from Nice to Marseille, and the Germans were now pulling back across the Seine. The Russians too were adding to the squeeze on the Fatherland and had advanced to the East Prussian Frontier while De Gaulle had made a triumphant re-entry into Paris.

The Spitfire IX had appeared in 1943 and the FW 190 was no longer having it all its own way. Although the Yanks were taking murderous punishment in their big Flying Fortresses they were latterly being escorted by the new wonder fighter the Mustang, powered by the Rolls Royce engine. With its wing drop-tanks and enormous inboard petrol tanks giving it a seven-hour endurance, this new fighter could escort the Forts right up to the German frontier. It was the first genuine long-range fighter, a type which the British themselves had never had during the war.

The Hurricane, armoured with cannon and 250lb bombs, was still going strong and proving itself afresh as a tactical ground support aeroplane. With the Typhoon, it seemed the likeliest option to everyone. I hoped it would be the Hurricane.

CHAPTER 21

Joan had finally been persuaded to visit her sister and the new baby in Kent and had taken off the previous weekend for ten days. Although I was happy about this, I was disturbed without being able to identify the reason. The flying was going well and I was enjoying Ternhill; the boys were all extremely friendly, particularly the Canadians and the messing arrangements were very good. Why then this uneasy feeling? There was the question of the next posting of course and the posting after that. Obviously I wished I knew where that would be - and then I would worry about what Joan would do when that time came. "If only tomorrow could look after itself..." But that was always my problem. I am a born pessimist. I know the worst always happens and therefore worry about it and live all of its dire consequences in advance.

Anyway, following my Cosford experience I was casually on the lookout for the WAAF who had invited me to go to Shrewsbury one weekend, although I knew I would never have the nerve to do such a thing – not with a complete stranger, that is. But she was a very interesting girl and perhaps a drink with her one evening would be legitimate? Although I stared into every WAAF-driven car, van and truck that went past I never did see her again. However, I had a letter that morning from Marie in which she asked when I thought she might see me again. It caught me at a very vulnerable moment and I wrote back saying I would drive over early this coming Saturday. "I won't have another chance of seeing her," I reasoned, "and I've got to sort this out before I'm shipped off somewhere."

I left camp on the Saturday morning, too early even for breakfast and arrived in Bedford just before nine. Marie was expecting me and told me she was preparing our lunch as a picnic and did I mind if we spent the day in the country somewhere? What a stupid question.

It was a glorious day, the sun blazing out of the August sky, burnished and brassy, but we lay cool in the shade of a tree, just the two of us with the drone of insects on the faint breeze.

"Do you realize, we've known each other for seven years now?"

"Ever since I was a young schoolgirl - you cradle-snatcher. But that's a very abstract thought on a day like this. What brought it on?"

"I don't know." She looked so marvellous, the sun highlighting her golden hair. Conversation was unnecessary really, it was enough to just sit and be happy. But I wanted to say "I love you enormously, I always have," but I couldn't say it. The words stuck in my throat somehow.

"Now you look worried," and Marie put out her hand to touch my face, her own expression gentle as if she knew what I was thinking. We kissed contentedly and then passionately.

It was a wonderful day. We ate the sandwiches she had brought and drank the tea from a thermos and occasionally took sips of orange juice which by now was quite tepid. Then we laid back on the rug, with Marie snuggled up in my shoulder, content and sleepy. I hugged her, rejoicing in the warmth of her body through her thin blouse.

The evening cool finally brought us back to an awareness of things more practical than our day-long self-indulgence and I watched happily as Marie leaned into the back of the car to fuss with the picnic plates and boxes. With her grey cotton skirt immodestly high she caught my gaze and laughingly asked if I was going to lie there looking up her legs for the rest of the night. "I'd love to, but I've got better ideas," and I got up off the rug and started tickling her until she squirmed free, protesting and pleading.

We drove homewards in the gathering dusk. Marie directed me carefully along the way and then finally saying, "Look, over there. You can park there," indicating a track leading off the road. I happily drove up into the secluded lay-by. We got into the back of the car, but as I started kissing her she pulled away from me. I watched surprised as she began to unbutton her blouse and then unclasping her bra, slide the straps over her shoulders and down her arms inside the sleeves of her blouse. "I can't afford you tearing my undies. I haven't any clothing coupons left." She smiled challengingly. I mumbled something about 'escapology', but was actually too amazed to say anything sensible. However, I soon overcame my surprise and pulled her back into my arms.

It was a long, intensely passionate night, as though the years had rolled away and we were both back in our teens, very much in love and lost in each other. The rest of the world with all its problems, constraints, inhibitions, no longer featured. All that mattered was the now soft, sensuous bodies, the nestling almost greedy feeding upon each other, the breathless explorations, the hot demanding and ecstatic compliance - such as I had not experienced since those early days. Nature drove us on. She laid across my legs, her knees upon the seat beside me while my hand wandered over the contours of her body.

After awhile she pulled away from me and sat up, staring down at her hands in her lap. Then in answer to my unspoken protest - "It's not you I'm afraid of - it's me." and she buried her face in my chest and began to cry softly.

On the journey back to Bedford Marie sat quietly beside me, holding my hand tightly, occasionally dabbing at her eyes with a very screwed up handkerchief. It was three o'clock. We both felt tired and emotionally drained.

"I'll be in touch." I said as I drove away.

Fortunately, there was lots of flying over the next few days, gunnery, navigation and cross country trips and I even flew over and landed at Braunston one afternoon. Everyone came out from the crew room on to the apron to watch this Miles Master squeeze into the tiny airfield. It was a bit of a line shoot really. I was otherwise very confused and miserable. Nothing had been resolved by my visit to Bedford which now seemed like a dream - one which left me feeling both guilty and wretched.

CHAPTER 22

1945

It was while aerobatting with my instructor that I once again experienced the pain in my head on trying to lose height. This was the third time it had happened although only the second time I had to report sick with it. The medical officer proposed to send me up straight away to the RAF Hospital at Cleveleys, near Blackpool.

"There's little point in repeating the treatment you had last time at Cosford. We must find out the cause rather than simply treating the effect."

"Come on doc, please. I'll miss all the flying again and anyway, the course is nearly over." The Medical Officer shook his head as if to say "Why do they always argue?"

"Look, I've had a bit of a cold," I lied. "I should have gone sick - I promise I will next time."

"Next time you might not be so lucky and you'll run out of petrol before you can land. I'm sorry Berry, you're going to Cleveleys." The MO shrugged and turned away. Although convinced he was making mountains out of molehills I resignedly packed a bag and returned to the Sick Bay for the transport the MO had promised.

Cleveleys came as a very pleasant surprise. It was an opulently-appointed hotel on the promenade converted to serve as an officers' hospital and rehabilitation centre. It had the ambience of an exclusive London Club. There were some comfortably furnished wards each with three or four beds, although most of the patients were up and about. The messing arrangements were extremely civilised and the whole place was run, I imagine, like a high quality seaside nursing home.

One of the first patients I met was Flight Lieutenant Alan Bloom, also from Ternhill, who had been referred to Cleveleys with a stomach ulcer. He gave me the low-down on the hospital. Most of the 'inmates' apparently were aircrew suffering from various physical ailments as well as some from serious burns gained in flying accidents. Their stay was more like a holiday than a hospital.

I was given a thorough examination, X-rays, the lot, the next morning and told to go and rest up and to take it easy for a few days. Blackpool, a few yards down the road from Cleveleys, was in the middle of its summer holiday season, so it was obviously the place to go and explore. Alan and I wandered up and down the promenade and were astonished by the peacetime atmosphere which pervaded the place. It seemed as if the war-battered British were taking time out to recuperate. And who could blame them? For a few days the war was to be forgotten, forgotten that is until one tried to eat. Rationing continued in Blackpool of course, just as it did elsewhere and the holiday makers had to hand over their ration books to their landladies who then served the same powdered eggs and spam as they got at home. But fun was the major item on the menu and all the side shows, slot machines and the pier were still there, the paddling in the surf and of course the Tower and the trams. The only difference in the scene, apart from the absence of ice cream, was the blackout which effectively closed the place down after dark.

After the doctor's rounds in the mornings it was clear that we walking wounded could do as we pleased. The weather was hot and sunny and it was the choice of many of the patients to take a blanket out on to the sand and to sunbathe. Some of the patients receiving long term treatment for burns spoke of the amazing skill of their surgeon, a Dr MacKindo, who specialised in skin grafts and the rebuilding of faces following the most horrific flying accidents. The sight of these terribly disfigured men making so little of their suffering made me feel a complete cheat. I felt quite fit after all and with no outward signs of the problem that had brought me to the hospital. However, I had not asked to come, so I tried to be fatalistic about it, much as one did about most things in the RAF.

I went with Alan into Blackpool after dinner and, determined to sample all that the resort had to offer, we finished up in the Winter Garden Fairground. It was all very noisy with the various rides rumbling and the screams from the teenagers adding to the general cacophony.

The success of the rides seemed to be judged by the volume of shrieks they could produce from the young girls riding them. We were very amused, in fact, by the attention we were getting from a couple of these teenagers, two girls who were obviously trying to pick us up. They followed us around and contrived to pop up in front of us every so often, their smiles an open invitation. I was not into cradle-snatching, however, and dragged Alan away.

I saw the Medical Officer the next morning who again poked and peered into me and then told me to carry on taking things easy. We sat on the beach that afternoon dozing in the hot sun only to look up at a particularly loud shriek from some child as it was swung out over the waves by dad. "You *will* enjoy yourself - or I'll drown you!" muttered Alan.

Neither of us said anything again for a long time. Then Alan broke in upon my thoughts. "What's the problem?" Alan was peering at me. "No problem. Why do you ask?"

"You look worried and this is not the time or the place to worry. So, what are you worrying about? Women?" I sniggered nervously, surprised by Alan's apparent insight. I thought hard for a moment, tempted to confide in him.

"As a matter of fact I have got a problem, Alan - and it is about women - two of them."

"God, that's two too many, you poor old thing." He settled back in his deck chair, his eyes closed. "Tell your Uncle Alan all about it then."

I told him the whole story, how I had met this girl before the war and how we had both fallen in love very seriously, spending an idyllic three years until she had been evacuated at the start of the blitz on London; then how things had gone wrong and how I later met my wife-to-be. I then told of how I had met Marie again and had felt all the old passions return.

"I was too bloody infatuated and happy to tell the girl that I was now married and somehow I convinced myself that I could have both my cake and eat it. There was a war on and - hell - you know the drill." I grew fierce in my self-defence.

"I really don't old boy, but I can see your problem. So, now you've got to do the honourable thing - ask your wife if you can have a mistress." I looked at him witheringly.

"OK. In a perfect world I'd have both of them, but it isn't a perfect world - and I also know what the honourable thing is to do. But that's going to be painful for everyone." Alan looked at me quizzically, saying nothing. "Isn't life a bugger? I have this great physical thing with one, but God knows, she could be hell to live with - and real compatibility with the other, but without the sex."

"It's the old, old conflict between nature and society, old boy. One urges you to dip your wick whenever you can and the other says it's naughty. The ideal, of course, would be great compatibility and great sex with the same person." He looked thoughtful for a moment and then added, "I wonder if that's possible?"

"Well, yes, of course it is. Finding it is the problem though. And if you found it, I wonder if the sex bit would last?" It was my turn to look thoughtful.

"Sex is just another basic drive - nothing to do with emotions - just like eating. You eat when you're hungry and no one gets excited about it."

"You can't separate sex and emotion. No one can."

"I'm talking about basic sex, the sort that drives men to prostitutes."

"I wouldn't know about that, Alan. You make it all sound very animal."

"So, we're animal. Look at you last night, chasing schoolgirls." He leered at me as he continued through my protest. "You don't have to balk at the notion of sex being so basic; you can refine it if you want to make an occasion out of it - just as you can with eating - haute bonking if you like." I shook my head. "That's a gross over-simplification."

"So, why can't you have casual sex when you're hungry, without it being a crime, as well as enjoying a good fuck with the woman you're emotionally involved with? One doesn't have to preclude the other." Alan paused thoughtfully. "It's a pretty standard way of life for many men anyway - always has been."

"You are disgusting, Alan. What about the woman's viewpoint?"

"Oh, I'm sorry. The same rules apply to them of course."

There was silence for awhile as I tried to digest the implications of this. There were so many reasons why free love could not work; the whole question of bringing up the kids that might result, the question of loyalty to one person, and then there was the question of keeping emotions out of sex anyway, which would be a total impossibility - certainly impossible for me. Society would fall apart!

"Mankind can become animal enough, at the drop of a hat, without making it easier for it to happen. You have to have some moral constraints for society to operate at all. Cats legitimately hunt and kill mice, but that doesn't give us the right to hunt and murder people. And what about all the bastards that would be produced if free love were normal?"

"Yes, that is a problem I agree. But, say they invent a pill which is a hundred per cent effective in preventing conception. What then?"

"Come on Alan. What happens now if the lads forget to carry a French letter? Does it stop them from having it off? Of course it doesn't! You're simply preaching self-indulgence when we should be struggling to rise above the animals. And what about the woman's point of view too? "

"Bull shit! I'm trying to help you come to terms with your guilty conscience, that's all." Alan grinned at me.

"So, you don't really believe in this free love then - all this crap you've been giving me?"

"Yes I do, in fact. And it will all happen just as I say one day - I only hope I live that long!"

I shook my head in disbelief. "You're forgetting the church in this Alan, among a thousand other moral and ethical points."

"Ah now, that raises another one of my theories..." But I heaved myself up out of my chair, raising my hands up to the heavens. "Let's go and have dinner."

After three more days of the Cleveleys' experience, I was posted back to Ternhill and reality. I reported to the medical officer as I had been told to do, giving him the letter I had brought back from Cleveleys and expecting to be cleared for flying once more. The MO read the report and then looked up at me. "You're not going back to flying - yet anyway. You're going to have a medical board first."

"What the hell does that mean?"

"You know what a medical board is - you've had them before." The Medical Officer was very patient.

"Yes, I know. But why should I have a medical board?"

"To establish your status for flying." I groaned and swallowed my remark about red tape. "When will this be then?"

"It will take a few days to set up no doubt, but you will be notified."

It took only three days in fact, before I was told to report to the Sick Bay. The MO went off without comment and I found myself sitting before a sombre, white-haired officer. Group Captain Dickson cleared his throat and peered over the top of his glasses at me. "I am afraid that you are to be re-categorised and taken off flying."

I was shattered. I stared at the Group Captain for long moments before I could say anything. It was a totally unexpected verdict. I had had no inkling that I might be grounded - given some course of treatment perhaps and even relegated back to the next course having missed so much of this one. But to be grounded. It was impossible.

"But Sir, this thing has only ever happened a couple of times when I have been flying at altitude."

The Group Captain explained patiently that no one could take the risk that it might happen again - no, would happen again - when I would be unable to get down. "In these circumstances I fear you are no longer fit to fly operationally." He closed the file on his desk, but I seized upon the phrase - no longer fit to fly operationally.

"Could I not continue flying non-operationally? This condition only happens if I go above 10,000 or so feet and one never has to go above 6,000 when you are instructing, indeed 5,000 would be more

172

accurate. Could I not continue instructing, Sir?" Dickson stared hard at me for some moments.

"You want to continue flying, Berry?" I nodded emphatically. "It would be a great pity to waste all my training Sir, particularly since I would still be able to do it medically."

The Group Captain re-opened the file and unscrewed the top of his pen. "I'm re-categorising you as Non-operational, below 5,000 feet. Satisfied?"

Confirmation of re-categorisation, 27th February 1945

CHAPTER 23

Shortly after the medical board my posting came through - back to Desford! For the third time in my relatively short Air Force career I was posted to this station. Renowned for being obtuse, if not bloody-minded even, the Air Force could always be guaranteed to get it wrong, like posting the boilermaker into parachute packing, or the Cornish miner to Carlisle. Not that I minded if, for once, someone in Group had got it right. It would have been difficult at that time to have found a better posting in the entire Air Force. The gazetting of my promotion to Flying Officer, which fortuitously greeted me on my return in September 1944, did little to offset my mounting conviction that something terrible must be pending. Bad things always happen in threes.

In many ways it was a great disappointment to return to flying Tiger Moths once again. In spite of all the future uncertainties involved at Ternhill, the flying had been exciting and the prospect of flying operational types like the Typhoon, both scary and challenging. Mastering these powerful, deadly aeroplanes occupied me fully at the time, leaving little room for the thought of fighting for life in them. If ever I had felt vulnerable it was on account of aircraft reliability and not because of thoughts of the enemy, or even of my own fallibility. I think that was a fairly standard attitude - and probably just as well.

Flying Tigers once again seemed far less relevant, even though I had pleaded for the option. At Desford we were currently involved in acclimatising Canadian trained pilots to fly in the UK. In Canada, pilot navigation appeared to consist of finding a railway line and flying along it until you got to a town. In this country such pilots became hopelessly lost once airborne. So, flying was restricted mainly to navigational exercises and cross country flights and excluded the excitement, such as it was, of getting someone off solo, or of falling out of the sky attempting an as-yet-uninvented aerobatic. The monotony of such flying was broken occasionally when a visitor would bring some unusual aircraft type on to the field and could be persuaded to give the boys a ride. I missed out on a Lancaster, and the Blenheim which the already famous Wing Commander Guy Gibson flew in one day, although I did get a trip in a De Havilland Rapide, a veteran twin-engined biplane with an enclosed cabin holding five passengers. It cruised steadily at about 135 mph and was very easy to fly, a bit like a twin-engined Tiger Moth, only cosier. They still fly them, half a century later, on local routes, of course.

Before I left Ternhill, and after my conversation on the topic with Alan Bloom, I wrote to Marie Roche and told her that I was married. It was a letter full of regrets and apologies and a plea for her understanding. I told her that I had always loved her and how that fact had blinded me to the ultimate hurt it would cause to her - and my wife. "If only things had been different ... If only things could still be different?"

I left the question in the air, I guess unable even then to finalise it. It hurt me to write the letter and I know it must have hurt her too. But the war would be over one day and it did look now as if I would survive it. It was an impossible situation and one could not allow it to continue, no matter how much the hurt. I told her I was returning to Desford and that if she ever wanted to get in touch with me to write to me there. I hoped she would write, not because I wanted to carry everything on, but because I desperately wanted to have her reaction. She never did write.

I had ten days leave at Christmas and we motored down to Sittingbourne. We spent the first few days with my family, including Christmas Day and then went down to Joan's for Boxing Day. Both families were delighted that I was no longer going on to operational flying and, in view of the way the war was developing in Europe, felt able to start talking about our future.

"Thank God for the way things have turned out," Mum said. "I wish you were off flying altogether though." I suppose I had a hazy idea just how much my family worried about me, but I would need a child of my own one day fully to appreciate the worries and even heartaches they can bring. As it was I felt a slight impatience with Mum and Dad over their fussings and concerns.

"Will you come back to Sittingbourne when this is all over?" "I don't know Mother. I doubt it. I certainly will not be going back t'Mill." I smiled at her hoping to lighten the conversation, but knowing only too well that we would never be coming back. "I could try to get in to civil aviation, but I guess thousands of ex-RAF types will have the same idea. The other option is architecture. But heavens knows if I could swing that one."

"I'm sure you could, dear. It would be so much safer than this awful flying."

The war news was as optimistic as it had ever been. By the previous September MacArthur had returned to the Philippines, the Allies had breached the Siegfried Line and the Germans had been in full retreat across Europe. There was now a perceptible shift away from just 'grim survival today' towards 'what of tomorrow?'. People were beginning to ask, "What happens when this is all over?" Perhaps, surprisingly, the politicians were already ahead of the people in this regard, for Beveridge had already produced his Report heralding the post-war welfare state two years previously, in December 1942!

So it was on an unusually optimistic note that we returned off leave to Leicester. The decision at this time that I should be put up for re- categorisation of my instructor's rating also gave a new objective to my flying. I went up regularly over the next few weeks with Squadron Leader Cope, the present deputy CFI, for patter and flying practice. Then the Chief Flying Instructor himself, Squadron Leader Wardell, took an interest in my flying. Wardell was a perfectionist and demanded the highest possible performances, regardless of the weather, for most of the flights with him were in black flag conditions when everyone else was grounded.

In February a Flight Lieutenant Cleife, from the Central Flying School at Hullavington, arrived on the station for the test. It lasted an hour and on completion, as we walked back across the tarmac to the control tower, Cleife congratulated me and told me I was now category 'A2'. This was duly recorded in my logbook with the rating of an 'above average instructor and pilot.'

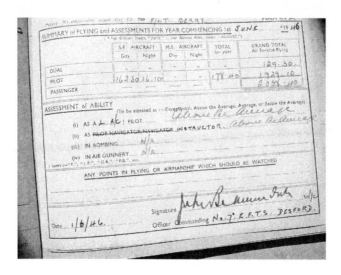

Log book entry, June 1946

Spring saw the war in Europe reaching its cataclysmic climax. Although defeated in everything but name, the Germans continued to fight driven on by the manic Hitler from his bunker in Berlin. The call for unconditional surrender, which the Allies had set at their Yalta conference, was also undoubtedly prolonging the agonies of the armies converging upon Berlin. And then, as the Russian T.52 tanks closed in upon the threshold of Hitler's bunker beneath the Chancellery, the news erupted that he was dead. This was followed by the ignominious hanging of Mussolini and his mistress from lampposts in Milan. It was all over - at least as far as the war in Europe was concerned - and Churchill's "Iron Curtain" was about to descend upon a still-troubled world.

As far as I was concerned this period saw the diminution of my flying. Although ab initio instruction had resumed after the acclimatisation flying of the Canadians, now it all seemed a bit pointless. I flew 65 hours in March, but this had reduced to only 25 hours by the following August. Not that the CFI had given up trying to hound us into the air, but for veterans like me it all seemed unnecessary. By virtue of my status as an A2 instructor however, I was now spending quite a bit of time testing pupils for their first solos in both day and night flying, as well as testing aircraft coming out from their 500-hour service. Not all of them were perfectly rigged after the event of their virtual rebuild and some did fly, well - oddly.

I also landed another chore, one which I always enjoyed - weather testing. On those days when the cloud base seemed to be near deck level and it was a toss-up as to whether flying was possible or not, someone had to go up to test it and, if necessary, wash-out flying.

I loved the drama on those mornings of near clampdown, of being the only aeroplane to break the silence and to taxi out into the fog for a circuit at 30 feet or so. Without any wind, and with no other aeroplanes out there, the take-off would be straight from the hangar apron and the circuit flown within the perimeter of the airfield. Knowing that everyone in the dispersals would be watching, a sideslip landing back on the hangar apron was de rigour - so that the ground staff hardly had to move to grab the wing tips and to guide me back into the hangar. A muffed landing in front of such a critical and expert audience was unthinkable.

The other option was when the windsock was being torn from its mast by gale-force winds and someone had to go up to see if even dual flying was at all possible. That I enjoyed less. The ground staff would line up like a mini-landing path and coming in between them at 60, into a gale of 30, or 40+ mph, meant that they could catch and hold your wings soon after you had touched down without having to run very far, or fast.

With the reduced number of pupils now coming through the system and the resultant reduction in the amount of flying, the satellite field at Braunston became redundant and the two flights located there were brought back to the parent aerodrome. All of the aeroplanes had to be ferried out and I had the dubious honour of flying out the last one. This rather melancholy act was a prelude to a whole series of flights which followed over the rest of the summer. As the training programme shrank so the number of aircraft required was reduced and the surplus were flown to various graveyards for some unknown fate. Two instructors would take an aeroplane each to destinations like Brough, Kirkbride, Carlisle or St Athen and, leaving one of the planes behind, the two would return in the second one.

No 7 EFTS Officers' Mess, RAF Desford, 1945

In the late summer a new personality appeared on the station called the Group Education Officer. His role was to advertise the new facilities to be offered to all personnel to advise and prepare them for their return to civilian life. The Educational and Vocational Training Scheme, as it was to be called, also referred to grants to be made available for undertaking certain vocational and professional courses on demobilisation. I was knocking on the door of the EVT man as soon as I heard about it and it did sound possible that a grant would be made available for the study of architecture.

This was a matter of far greater concern to me, at this stage, than was flying. I made great friends with the Group Education Officer while he was with us and over the next two weeks spent every spare minute I could with him discussing how the scheme should and could be implemented on the station. This made the job of the Group Education Officer so much simpler and he welcomed my help with enthusiasm! He had a temporary office in the admin block just down the corridor from the CO's office. Wing Commander Beaumont was fully aware of what was happening and gave his approval to whatever was going on. This meant that the Adjutant, without actively supporting us, did not get in the way either. In the end, and in the absence of anyone else who knew anything about the scheme, after the Group man left I became the Station Education Officer.

Within weeks I had commandeered the use of a large room in the admin block which I equipped with desks, chairs, visual aids and decorated with numerous EVT posters sent down from Group. I was now in business lecturing and advising candidates on their future careers in civvy street. This, of course, was done in accordance with the prescribed practices as laid down in the many pieces of 'bumph' sent down from on high. A particular event however, was the visit from Group of an occupational psychologist. He came down to administer psychological aptitude tests designed to determine the most suitable occupations for the candidates. A few of the instructors and ground staff took the tests, not because they wanted to find out their most appropriate occupation, but more to find out what the hell occupational psychologists were. I took the tests as well, but with a much more serious intention. I really did want to know what job might best suit me. I was told that I should either go into the merchant navy - or become an architect!

1946

Occasionally the Group man would call at the station to check on developments and to bring down the latest bundle of careers posters. He seemed to be very happy with my organisation and presumably said as much to the Commanding Officer on his visits, because that great man would nod and smile indulgently whenever he put his head round the door. This indulgence was not shared, however, by the Chief Flying Instructor. Whenever Squadron Leader Wardell saw me in the admin block he would start to rant about my flying, or lack of it.

"You only did eleven hours last month Berry. What the hell are you doing? The only way I can get you into the air these days is put you in charge of night flying, or send you up on a weather test."

"Yes Sir. I am trying to implement this EVT Scheme, Sir, as you know."

"EVT - bollocks! You're a flying instructor, not a bloody wingless wonder. If you don't get into the air I shall have to talk to the CO." It was immediately after this particular confrontation that the CO put his head round the door and gave me a large wink. He had obviously heard Wardell's outburst.

"Why the hell doesn't he say something to Wardell and get me off the hook?" I couldn't understand what the problem was, although I began to suspect that he had, anyway, because the CFI usually had half a smile even while he was tearing me off a strip and there never was any follow-up to his threats. I began to think that I was probably the subject of an ongoing joke between the Old Man and the CFI. "What the hell - this is the most important thing happening today," and I got on with my efforts which were quite unique in my service experience and therefore very enjoyable.

By now I had my second ring up - as a Flight Lieutenant - and the CFI meanwhile had found another way of getting me airborne. He sent me up to give patter practice to some of my colleagues, much as he had tutored me for my re-categorisation. The Commanding Officer too found another role for me, that of scrounger. Among my other innovations in the admin block I had started building a photographic darkroom. I had one of the ground staff in the hangar construct an enlarger, an amazing structure, out of triangulated timbers with the enlarger head sliding up and down on strings. The CO, also an amateur photographer, encouraged me to do this and kept an interested watch on progress. I was finally held up minus a safe light and the necessary dishes.

"The MU (Maintenance Unit) at Coventry must have dozens of such things. Go over there and see what you can scrounge." The Wing Commander made it sound like an everyday activity. I was not so sure although I knew that such things did go on. The service scrounger was a legendary type after all, though more often found in fiction than in fact. He was usually an NCO, but sometimes featured as a junior officer. I had never pictured myself as either. The MU at Coventry was an old peacetime establishment and I recalled seeing its enormous hangars from the air often enough. "How the hell do I break in to a place like that and ask if I can have a developer dish? They'll think I'm round the bend."

I booked myself out and flew over towards Coventry. The MU was on the north side of the city, only a few minutes flying time from Desford. I circled the field at 1,500 feet and identified that it was a right-hand circuit before lowering down to join it and then to land. An airman waved me in, which solved the first problem as to where I should report. I dumped my parachute and helmet in the rear cockpit, put on my forage cap and followed the airman to the control tower. The Duty Pilot asked for my signature and the purpose of my visit.

"Ah ... yes. I'm hoping to collect some photographic equipment.''

"Yes Sir. Have you been here before?"

"No. Where do I go?"

The Duty Pilot shrugged his shoulders and looked vaguely around the office.

"I haven't a clue. I was hoping you would know."

I began to feel depressed. I didn't want to get involved in discussions about what Photographic Equipment I was supposed to be collecting.

"Well, where does one usually go?" It sounded stupid, but I thought it was quite intelligent. The Duty Pilot must have thought so too because, frowning hard, he then gave me directions to the Main Stores building as he called it. My spirits sank lower and lower as I trekked around what I found to be a very large establishment. It all looked very unfriendly and not the sort of place to start one's scrounging career. I found the Main Stores, identifying it from the faded lettering over its entrance. It was a huge warehouse building with internal proportions which lost themselves in gloom. Vast racks of objects rose upwards to an almost invisible ceiling and a Hausman-like gridiron of alleyways disappeared in their perspectives.

An NCO, stripes pinned temporarily to greasy overalls, appeared after a few moments to ask what I wanted. Now, it was here that the legendary scrounger would have come out with his remarkable, but convincing, story. I however, was defeated before I started. I had no confidence whatever in my ability to bullshit this airman and no prearranged story which might have got half a hearing.

"I come from Desford - Number 7 EFTS - where we are trying to build a photographic darkroom. The only equipment I've got so far is the enlarger and I'm looking for everything else, dishes, safelights, developing tanks, a clock and of course, chemicals. Can you help me please?" I put my hands on the counter and beamed encouragingly at the impassive NCO.

"Not without the necessary requisitions, Sir. Have you got an authority?" I shook my head.

"No. This is all very informal, but my CO thinks that a darkroom would give us greater efficiency in our flying instruction." My imagination was beginning to work, if creakily. "The war could be over before we got the necessary authority from Group and we need the stuff now." The NCO looked even more depressed than I actually felt. He shook his head slowly. "What sought of stuff do you want?" I repeated the list, losing heart rapidly, adding lamely, "Anything really."

The NCO turned away and disappeared into the depths of the Stores. My heart rose as I began to imagine him coming back with his arms full of equipment. Perhaps this scrounging business was not so hard after all. My optimism was dashed however, when I saw the airman return to place on the counter two small developing dishes and a developing tank - without its spiral. "That's the best I can do for you without a proper requisition."

Back at Desford, Wing Commander Beaumont was not very impressed.

CHAPTER 24

It hardly seemed possible. After five dark and foreboding years of war, peace was like emerging from an awful nightmare and waking to find the sun shining and everything normal after all. A sense of achievement and relief underlay most peoples' feelings, as if a good job had been well done. The mood was of great optimism for the future. The fruits of victory, however, began to look a bit over-ripe as the winter deepened and rationing was reintroduced on a wartime scale. The socialist government, after an astonishing victory at the polls last summer, was now confronted by the effects of a world food shortage and the need to feed thirty million Germans following the destruction of their agricultural industry. This was a disappointing result for a people who had just won a war - not that I noticed any difference in the way I was eating. Perhaps the most disturbing news for the members of the mess was the subsequent announcement that beer production was to be cut - by up to 50%! The fact that bananas were once more returning to the shops was no great compensation either. As the summer advanced so the food situation worsened; meat was down to 1/- worth per week - a drop of 2d - there was no petrol for pleasure motoring and no foreign travel for holidays. As Clement Attlee said, "The sacrifice was akin to wartime."

For me, peace brought little change, it seemed. I only did 20 hours flying in the first six months of the year, averaging 3.3 hours per month, most of which was night flying. The CFI said this was the only way to get me into the air.

Two or three Air Force Crosses and Air Force Medals, AFC's and AFM's, were awarded each year on the station. These usually went to the Flight Commanders, with a very few AFM's to non-commissioned officers. The AFC, a peacetime gong, was awarded for acts of courage and devotion to duty when flying. In the case of the flying instructors it was usually in recognition of their 'devotion to duty' as represented by the amount of instructional hours flown. No way did I begrudge the honour bestowed on these men, indeed I always thought of them as being extremely well deserved. To sit in the front seat of a Tiger Moth for five hours every day, week after week, month after month and even year after year; going through the same routines, suffering the same risky landings and all with the same eternal patience, was the stuff from which super-beings were made. Justifiably, I knew I would never qualify even with my 2,000 hours on Tiger Moths alone! Someone did say to me once "If you put half the effort into your flying as you put into that EVT business, you'd be sporting a gong by now.".

The current crop, however, involved what I thought was a great injustice. One of the Flight Commanders, a personal friend of mine, the most conscientious, sincere and devoted of men to his duty was only 'mentioned in dispatches' and awarded the little bronze Oak Leaf to wear beneath his brevet. Tommy Benstead never complained of course, he was far too modest and sincere about his job.

My zeal in implementing the EVT scheme on the station was not wholly altruistic of course. Ever since the possibility of post-war grants for ex-servicemen had been mooted, I had kept as close as I could to the scheme, determined to grab whatever opportunities came up and I applied for such a grant just as soon as the details arrived on the station. It was a long shot, I felt, and I hardly dared to think about it as a possibility.

I had already made contact with the School of Architecture in the Leicester College of Art and Technology and had met the Head of School - Frank Chippindale. The interview had gone extremely well and Frank Chippindale had said that in view of my maturity and war service I could enter straight into the second year of the five-year course - if I got a grant!

"I'll never get a grant," I moaned and even though Joan secretly agreed, she never fed my pessimism. "Oh, come on. Cross the bridges as you get to them. If they are available why shouldn't you get one?"

"4,999 reasons if there is only one grant and 5,000 apply for it. Look, they aren't going to give them to every Joe that applies."

"How do you know?" and then realising that this was a weak sort of reply, she quickly added, "There's nothing to gain in being defeatist. Yours must have been one of the first applications they received and you are probably quite well known at Group by now. I bet Flight Lieutenant What's-his-name - ?" "Roberts!" "Flight Lieutenant Roberts will put in a good report for you." How little she knew about the Air force!

I gave up, inwardly praying that Joan was right and not knowing just how soon her optimism was to be vindicated. The very next day I got the news that I had been awarded a grant of £468 per annum, payable on demobilisation, to cover the cost of a full time course in architecture. The news was stupendous and we celebrated that night by getting very drunk. It was not a fortune, but it would be enough to see us through, especially if Joan carried on working.

At last, it seemed as though the future was beginning to take shape. A local builder had bought the field beyond the end of Park Drive and was already digging foundations for half a dozen houses - semi-detached, three bedrooms plus garage space - speculative builder's versions. They were to sell at £850 and my grant would just about cover a 95% mortgage.

It was now May and demobilisation had begun. A few of the lads who had come in early in 1940 had already disappeared. I estimated that I might be out before the year ended and on the strength of that I went in to see Mr Chippindale again.

"Would you be willing to give me a provisional place for a start in September, on the assumption that I will be demobbed by then?" Frank Chippindale said he would be delighted to do just that.

"Provided you can start the course by mid October, I don't think it will matter too much if you miss the first few weeks. There will be half-a-dozen ex-servicemen starting this year and you will be joining about twenty young lads coming up from the first year." He looked thoughtful for a moment and then added, "I suppose that will be our problem - integrating the two age groups." He nodded as if to confirm his own thoughts. "It will be an interesting time."

The house would be ready by Christmas or thereabouts, so everything was falling neatly into place. The major snag would be if my demobilisation was delayed and I was not able to start the course in

October. It would waste an entire year and mean that I would have to find some temporary work to pay the mortgage.

For the first time I became aware of a certain paradox; on the one hand I was intensely impatient to get out and to start my new life as a student, but on the other hand I began to realise how much I would miss my present status - my Flight Lieutenant's uniform and those beloved wings over my breast pocket. An architectural student did not have quite the same cachet perhaps. Whatever doubts I had were quickly dispelled, however, whenever I thought about the future as a practising architect. It was a truly amazing opportunity and I felt very thankful for it.

It hadn't been a bad war for me!

Photograph courtesy of the Imperial War Museum, London

DENNIS BERRY

Following his demobilisation from the RAF in 1946, Dennis Berry did go on to study at Leicester School of Architecture. On qualifying in 1951, he worked for Sir Hugh Casson in London; one of his first assignments was assisting with the Festival of Britain.

The years from 1947 to his death in 2005 form the basis of the second instalment of Dennis's autobiography. Among other things, they include: forming his own practice, teaching at Kingston School of Art; racing Formula 750 cars; appointment to the Headship of Kingston School of Architecture; cats; the merger to form Kingston Polytechnic; cricket; the welcome arrival of Jonathan; studying then teaching with the Open University; Dean of Professional Studies; more cats; teaching *Modern Architecture* and *Creativity* to American students; writing five books; becoming the first Chair of The Groves Medical Centre Patients Group, then the first Chair of Kingston Hospital Patients Forum.

When Dennis wrote his curriculum vitae for the final time he headed it: *'Dennis Berry - architect, war-time flying instructor, writer and educationalist'*. If he had needed to write it again in the early years of 2000, he could have added *'patients' champion'*.

Dennis Berry died on 18th August 2005, aged 83.

INDEX TO PICTURES

Photographs courtesy of the Imperial War Museum, London

BOOKS BY
NUMBER 11 PUBLISHING

THE COBBOLD ELLISTON AFFAIR '... and the sin of the father shall be visited ...'
by Sandra Berry, published February 2007 ISBN 978-0-9555134-0-4

WHAT DID YOU DO IN THE WAR, DADDY? How did you help us to win?
by Dennis Berry, published September 2007 ISBN 978-0-9555134-1-1

TIME FOR CHANGE The Genesis of Modern Architecture
by Dennis Berry. To be published during 2008

FRANCIS EDWARD COBBOLD Sailor, Fijian Trader and Australian Pioneer Pastoralist
originally written in 1935 by Arthur W Upfield, edited by Sandra Berry for *The Cobbold Family History Trust*. To be published 2009

For a full list of Dennis Berry's paintings and how to obtain a copy,
write to   *Number 11 Publishing*
          PO Box 459
          New Malden
          Surrey KT3 9DH
or email: *no_11_publishing@blueyonder.co.uk*

For current information, check

www.number11publishing.co.uk
Books about interesting people – what they did, how they did it, and why